The Fugitive

TV Milestones

Series Editors
Barry Keith Grant
Brock University

Jeannette Sloniowski
Brock University

TV Milestones is part of the Contemporary Approaches to Film and Media Series

A complete listing of the books in this series can be found online at wsupress.wayne.edu

General Editor
Barry Keith Grant
Brock University

Advisory Editors
Robert J. Burgoyne
University of St. Andrews

Tom Gunning
University of Chicago

Caren J. Deming
University of Arizona

Thomas Leitch
University of Delaware

Patricia B. Erens
School of the Art Institute of Chicago

Anna McCarthy
New York University

Peter X. Feng
University of Delaware

Walter Metz
Southern Illinois University

Lucy Fischer
University of Pittsburgh

Lisa Parks
University of California–
Santa Barbara

Frances Gateward
Ursinus College

THE FUGITIVE

David Pierson

TV MILESTONES SERIES

Wayne State University Press   Detroit

© 2011 by Wayne State University Press,
Detroit, Michigan 48201. All rights reserved.
No part of this book may be reproduced without formal permission.

15 14 13 12 11   5 4 3 2 1

Library of Congress Cataloging-in-Publication Data

Pierson, David, 1958–
The fugitive / David Pierson.
p. cm. — (TV milestones)
Includes bibliographical references and index.
ISBN 978-0-8143-3429-4 (pbk. : alk. paper)
1. Fugitive (Television program) I. Title.
PN1992.77.F79P54 2011
791.43′72—dc23
2011019299

CONTENTS

ACKNOWLEDGMENTS vii

1. Man-on-the-Run 1

2. The Creation of *The Fugitive* 11

   Sources for the Series 14

   A Q.M. Production 18

   TV Programming and Cultural Influences 22

3. A Thematic Analysis of *The Fugitive* 41

   Individualism 42

   Love and Marriage 48

   Culture of Professionalism 56

   Modern Science and Technology 63

   Social Justice and Authority 66

4. The Legacy of *The Fugitive* 77

   The Fugitive: The Movie 90

   Coda 95

NOTES 97

WORKS CITED 99

FILM 105

TELEVISION 107

INDEX 111

ACKNOWLEDGMENTS

I would like to take this opportunity to thank a number of people who extended help, advice, and encouragement throughout the research and writing of this book. Special thanks go to Annie Martin at Wayne State University Press for her steadfast support, assistance, and patience in guiding me through the manuscript revision and publication processes. I would also like to thank the TV Milestones Book Series editors, Barry Keith Grant and Jeannette Sloniowski, for their insightful editorial suggestions on improving the overall style and flow of the manuscript, and to the two anonymous readers for their thoughtful and encouraging comments on early drafts of the book. I also would like to express my gratitude to the Press's Editorial Board and all the Press staff responsible for the production and marketing of this book.

Closer to home, I would like to thank my faculty colleagues (Dan, Russ, Lenny, Rebecca, Matt, Erika, Dennis, Maureen) in the Department of Communication and Media Studies, and former dean Devinder Malhotra of the College of Arts and Sciences at the University of Southern Maine for supporting this endeavor by approving my sabbatical leave in the spring of 2009. During the sabbatical, I was able to produce an initial draft of the manuscript and prepare for the revision process.

I began thinking and writing about *The Fugitive* in the early 1990s for my master's thesis in Radio-TV-Film at the University of North Texas in Denton. I started watching the series on the A & E (Arts and Entertainment) Network when it began showing reruns of the original episodes in the late afternoon. In viewing the episodes, I was struck by David Janssen's haunting performance as Richard Kimble, Barry Morse's relentless nature as Lieutenant Gerard, and the dark, nihilistic tone of the series. The program's semi-anthology structure provided the perfect stage for intense, dramatic character explorations. It is no wonder that most series' episodes feature performances from actors, such as Bruce Dern, Robert Duvall, Warren Oates, and Tuesday Weld, who would later become recognizable feature film actors. Today, viewing the series is like spotting the who's who in the Hollywood film and television industries in the 1960s and 1970s. My critical interest in *The Fugitive* led me to choose the series as the topic of my thesis. I would like to express my appreciation to my thesis supervisor and friend Steve Fore for his invaluable input and critical insights, along with Justin Wyatt and John Kuiper, my steadfast thesis committee members, for their advice and support. I also would like to thank the Wayne State University Press for providing me an avenue for reexamining this early work and encouraging me to delve much deeper into the contexts surrounding the creation of the series for the ABC Network, its influences on subsequent dramatic semi-anthology series, and the reasons why it remains popular and meaningful to audiences several decades after its original broadcast.

Finally, I cannot express enough gratitude to my wife, Carol. She also served as my first editor, providing practical advice and suggestions for improving revisions of the manuscript. Despite the fact that I spent too many weeknights and weekends working on the book, Carol never complained. Her love, patience, and unwavering support made the publication of this book possible.

Chapter 1
Man-on-the-Run

In the early 1960s, scores of viewers rushed to their TV sets on Tuesday evenings at ten o'clock to see how Richard Kimble would once again escape from the ever-tightening grip of the police who were pursuing him unjustly for the murder of his wife. Loyal viewers tuned in every week to find out which guest star Kimble would befriend and what type of dramatically charged situation he would find himself embroiled in. The prime-time series became popular with groups of college students living in dorms who affectionately called it "The Fuge." Men with hectic professional lives probably identified with Kimble, who struggled every week to achieve a small measure of freedom and personal happiness against a persistent barrage of outside forces. Women, in particular, were enamored with David Janssen's (Richard Kimble) tough exterior but vulnerable demeanor. His haunted, confused facial expressions and brooding charisma were certainly reminiscent of the late screen idol James Dean ("The Fuge" 1965). The ABC-TV series *The Fugitive*, which ran from September 1963 to August 1967, features the story of Dr. Richard Kimble, an innocent man from Stafford, Indiana, who is unjustly accused, convicted, and sentenced to death for the murder of his wife. *The Fugitive* is television's longest-running chase story.

Each episode begins with the image of a train barreling down the tracks at night as it transports Kimble to be executed at the state prison. Kimble is accompanied by Lt. Philip Gerard (Barry Morse), the man who arrested him for his wife's murder. William Conrad's somber but soothing voice introduces the prisoner's fate: "Proved guilty, what Richard Kimble could not prove was that the moment before he discovered his wife's body he encountered a man running from the vicinity of his home . . . a man with one arm. A man who has not been found." We then see a shot of Kimble inside the train, his face reflected in the compartment window as Conrad describes his limited future: "Richard Kimble ponders his fate as he looks at the world for the last time . . . and sees only darkness. But, in that darkness, fate moves its huge hand." In a sudden twist of fate, the train derails and Kimble is freed to begin his long cross-country search for the one-armed man. At the same time, he is doggedly pursued by the obsessive Gerard, who blames himself for Kimble's escape. Each episode is framed by Peter Rugolo's rousing theme music and is sequenced into the now familiar multiple act structure from prologue/opening to Act I through Act IV and the inevitable "epilogue" common to most Q.M. (Quinn Martin) Productions. Q.M. Productions' highly stylized structure lends each episode a sense of a theatrical, dramatic presentation and serves as a recognizable trademark for the production company.

The Fugitive offers viewers an unusual role reversal. While the convicted criminal is the series' hero, the hard-working, dedicated police protagonist is the show's villain. Gerard is at first a bureaucratic fussbudget who sees the world in simple black-and-white terms (Proctor 1994, 185). There is little room for moral ambiguity and uncertainty in his world. Gerard's character is a sly critique on the dispassionate Sgt. Joe Friday of the popular 1950s TV police drama series *Dragnet* (1951–59).

He also references the cool, technocratic bureaucrats who were part of Kennedy's New Frontier administration. New Frontier social liberalism insists that most social problems, like poverty, unemployment, and crime, can be addressed through applying scientific methods and bureaucratic procedures. Even though Gerard is only in about one in four episodes in the series, his intense presence can be felt even in episodes where he is absent. Despite his incontestable sense of duty, Gerard's character seems to grow slightly less intense and more humane over the course of the series. Morse's skillful and subtle performance prevents him from being a one-dimensional character. He confers on Gerard a degree of humanity beneath his shield of stoic professionalism.

Of course, for most viewers, the strongest appeal of *The Fugitive* is the memorable, poignant performance of Janssen as Richard Kimble. Janssen, a man of ordinary physical build and appearance, plays Kimble as a man who is capable of losing himself in a crowd and who can easily speak and act in an inconspicuous manner. Kimble is the type of person who can easily disappear if the situation demands it. David Thorburn points out that the physical authority of most male film stars, like Kirk Douglas or Burt Lancaster, would have been a huge impediment for the role. Janssen's low-key persona and demeanor make him a thoroughly credible character (Thorburn 1977, 192).

Janssen was born David Harold Meyer in Naponee, Nebraska, the son of Berniece Meyer, a former Ziegfeld girl. Before the series, the gruff-voiced actor with rather large ears was probably best known as the "leading man's best friend" in grade-B Hollywood movies. Janssen provides Kimble with a range of subtle psychological nuances expressed through minute movements, facial expressions, and vocal inflections (Thorburn 1977, 192). Because Kimble is always being pursued, Janssen plays him as a furtive man who can never really relax; even when he laughs or smiles, there is an undercurrent of nervousness. When Kimble spots a policeman, his back literally stiffens as an anxious expression darts across his face. Janssen invests Kimble with a strong measure of vulnerability. He has a gentlemanly demeanor and is resolute in the face of peril. Janssen's ability to make a haunted, introverted character the central dramatic focus for a weekly prime-time dramatic series is a testament to his acting talents.

The Fugitive is probably television's first true existential series. Because of his conviction and fugitive status, Kimble is socially alienated from most of his family and friends. He is unable to practice medicine without raising suspicion. Kimble must either stay on the run in search of the one-armed man who can clear him or accept his fate and face execution. Kimble's weekly Herculean toiling in menial jobs is reminiscent of Albert Camus's appropriation of the myth of Sisyphus to describe modern man's eternal and absurd struggle for meaning and unity in his life. Every time Kimble is close to finding the one-armed man, Fred Johnson, fate intervenes and the man escapes. Likewise, Gerard is equally frustrated by his inability to apprehend Kimble. For four years, these three men are caught in a surreal, dramatic cycle of chasing and evading one another across the geographic span of America.

As a fugitive, Kimble is free from normal social commitments; he has time to scrutinize his troubled past and to find his own personal redemption. His situation as an innocent man falsely accused and hunted for a crime he did not commit expresses the fear and paranoia associated with the cold war Red Scare and McCarthyism. The fugitive's status as a social outcast enables him to empathize and help people who are marginalized by society, whether a disaffected housewife, migrant farm worker, or a teenage boy struggling with his identity. Kimble's compassionate behavior reflects the empathy taking hold in America, as African Americans, women, and other marginalized groups began pushing for social equality (Zane 2007). Kimble's fall from suburban grace represents the tacit deep-seated fears

David Janssen as Dr. Richard Kimble in the ABC-TV series *The Fugitive*.

of a bustling middle-class America still riding high and enjoying the fruits of the postwar economic boom. *The Fugitive* introduced and presented a disconcerting character, a wandering, fearful loner, into the optimistic landscape of the New Frontier America. The television historians Harry Castleman and Walter Podrazik assert that the series "was a program ahead of its time, presenting the intense struggle of a truly alienated American, years before the phrase became popular" (1982, 170).

I argue in this book that *The Fugitive* is one of the most influential dramatic television series because it established the essential narrative and thematic features of what I call the contemporary nonviolent, wanderer-redeemer television tradition. Popular and successful, *The Fugitive* was immediately followed by a rash of program imitators, all of which were based on the premise of a man-on-the-run in search of adventure and redemption: *The Loner* (1965–66), a western, and *Run, Buddy, Run* (1966–67), a situation comedy parody of *The Fugitive*, on CBS; *Run for Your Life* (1965–68), a contemporary adventure, and *Branded* (1965–66), a western, on NBC; and *A Man Called Shenandoah* (1965–66), a western, on ABC (Brooks and Marsh 1988). *The Fugitive*'s influence, however, does not rest with merely spawning a parade of program imitators but in laying the mythic and narrative groundwork for the generations of wanderer-redeemer series that would follow it. The "contemporary" wanderer-redeemer differs from the popular television western hero because he does not exist in the historic past; he is "one of us," existing in our time period and addressing social issues relevant to the audience. While Kimble was not the first nonviolent, wanderer-redeemer on American television,[1] his character has the darkest criminal past (murder conviction), bleakest future (execution), and strongest drive for personal redemption. Roy Huggins, the series creator, asserted that *The Fugitive* was popular because its story centers on the universal themes of guilt and redemption, which are the quintessential themes in American literature and film (quoted in Glover and Bushman 2006, 70). Through its modern story of personal hardship and redemption, the series taps into the redemptive myths and beliefs that comprise America's Judeo-Christian cultures and traditions.

The Fugitive's long-term TV clout can be seen in the diverse range of prime-time contemporary wanderer-redeemer series that have followed it: *The Invaders* (1967–68), *Then Came Bronson* (1969–70), *The Immortal* (1970–71), *The Incredible Hulk* (1978–82), *The A-Team* (1983–87), *Highway to Heaven* (1984–89), *Starman* (1986–87), *Quantum Leap* (1989–93), *Renegade* (1992–97), *Touched by an Angel* (1994–2003), *Nowhere Man* (1995–96), *The Pretender* (1996–2000), *Promised Land* (1996–99), and *Prison Break* (2005–9). Several of these series mixed together the supernatural and the fantastic with the thematic of the wanderer-redeemer tradition. Each wanderer-redeemer series speaks to the societal needs and desires of the time period in which it was produced. *The Fugitive* provided a new narrative and thematic attribute to the tradition by featuring a nonviolent redeemer protagonist.

The Fugitive is also the first American dramatic series to feature a final, concluding episode. Before the series, only a handful of series, such as *The Howdy Doody Show* (1947–60) and *Leave It to Beaver* (1957–63), had concluding programs. Roy Huggins believed that *The Fugitive* should have a final episode; at first, Quinn Martin resisted the idea of producing one, fearing that it would undervalue the series' syndication profits. In the end, however, Martin agreed that *The Fugitive* should have a conclusion to satisfy its devoted audience. The resulting two-part final episode, "The Judgment" (8/22/67, 8/29/67), was seen by more people than any single episode of a regular series in the history of television up to that time (Robertson 1993, 173–80). There is little doubt that the series' loyal viewers were gratified and rewarded by the sight of Kimble leaving a courthouse, finally exonerated of the murder charges, hesitantly shaking hands with Gerard, and walking off to his new life. *The Fugitive* held its ratings record for thirteen years until the 1980 episode of *Dallas* in which J. R. Ewing's attacker was revealed. Shows that followed *The Fugitive*'s lead in presenting a popular and successful final episode included the *Mary Tyler Moore Show* (1970–77), *M*A*S*H* (1972–83), *Dallas* (1978–91), and *Cheers* (1982–93) (Robertson 1993, 14).

Unlike other television series that have quickly come and gone, *The Fugitive* retains a firm and secure place in our popular collective memory. It may be because the series' story of a lonely, dispossessed American wandering the countryside in search of redemption and a way to return home emotionally resonates with viewers decades after the series' original broadcast. Or it may be Janssen's haunting, enduring performance as Kimble. Or it may be because the series' dark fatalistic tone presents a sharp contrast to socially optimistic professional TV dramas from the era such as *The Defenders* (1961–65) and *Mr. Novak* (1963–65). *The Fugitive*'s popularity can be partly assessed in the sheer number of fan-based Web sites, online discussion groups, and publications devoted to the series. Because of its enduring popularity and influence on television culture, *The Fugitive* is one of television's true landmark dramatic series.

If parody can be understood as a form of flattery, *The Fugitive*'s status has made it a steady playful target for such TV programs as *It's the Garry Shandling Show* (1986–90), *Late Night with David Letterman* (1982–93), and *The Simpsons* (1989–present). By far, the cleverest parody is Chris Elliot's "The Fugitive Guy" skits on *Letterman* in 1985 in which he spoofs the series' Q.M. Productions opening with comically over-dramatized episode titles (e.g., "Tonight's Episode—A Pinch of Salt, a Dash of Death"). The film director David Lynch pays homage to the series by featuring a character named Philip Michael Gerard, a seemingly demonically possessed, one-armed shoe salesman, on ABC's *Twin Peaks* (1990–91). *The Fugitive* and *Twin Peaks* share a common interest in revealing the dark underbelly of idyllic small-town America. In Kimble's case, these small towns are often populated with corrupt sheriffs, duplicitous husbands, nosy neighbors, and prejudiced town folk.

The long-running series reappeared on television, cable this time, in the early 1990s when the cultural-centered Arts & Entertainment (A & E) Network began showing syndicated reruns in anticipation of Warner Brothers' planned release of a

1993 movie based on the series (A & E 1993, D-05). The movie proved to be a critical and financial success for the studio. The film stars Harrison Ford as Dr. Richard Kimble, Tommy Lee Jones as Gerard (Sam instead of Philip and a U.S. marshal rather than a police lieutenant), and Andreas Katsulas as the one-armed man, now called Fred Sykes instead of Fred Johnson. The film, directed by Andrew Davis, was nominated for several Academy Awards, including Best Picture. Jones won the award for Best Supporting Actor for his nuanced role as the clever, irascible Gerard. In the fall of 2000, CBS, attempting to recapture some of the magic from the original series, produced a television series remake of the same name. The series lasted only one season. It featured Tim Daly as Kimble, Mykelti Williamson as Gerard, and Stephan Lang as the one-armed man.

The Fugitive was not produced in a social and cultural vacuum. The series was created for ABC during a turbulent time when the three major TV networks were responding in force to charges made against them by federal regulators. These charges included making prime-time a "vast wasteland" of murder and mayhem to increasing juvenile delinquency through their violence-laden, action-adventure programs, such as ABC's *The Untouchables* (1959–63). *The Fugitive* was part of ABC's major programming initiative to produce new compassionate, dramatic adult programs that had less physical violence than action-adventure programs.

However, the series' road to prime-time was not a foregone conclusion. Chapter 2 examines the social, cultural, and programming influences on the creation of *The Fugitive,* along with the pivotal roles played by veteran TV producer-writer Roy Huggins and a relative newcomer producer, Quinn Martin. Chapter 3 explores the book's main question: why was *The Fugitive* was so popular with audiences in the 1960s? John Fiske argues that a television series is popular when there is an easy fit between the social discourses in the episodes and the social worlds of the viewers (1984, 169). Chapter 3 examines the dominant social discourses or themes that were prevalent in the series' episodes and in the social and cultural struggles taking place in early to mid-1960s American society. These themes include individualism, love and marriage, the culture of professionalism, modern science and technology, and justice and authority. I also maintain that many of these social conflicts and tensions still exist deep within the social and cultural fabric of American life. Chapter 4 looks at the legacy of the series and how it established the main narrative and thematic traits of the contemporary, nonviolent wanderer-redeemer television tradition. It argues that *The Fugitive* continues to have a strong influence on the generations of television wanderer-redeemer series that followed it. The chapter concludes with a discussion of the narrative and thematic differences between the series and the 1993 feature film version of *The Fugitive*.

Chapter 2
The Creation of *The Fugitive*

The Fugitive was almost never made. Roy Huggins, the series' creator, recalls the escalating tension and skepticism in a crowded hotel room filled with fifteen to twenty ABC network executives and programmers in 1962 as he explained his ideas for the series. Huggins said he flinched when ABC Network president Tom Moore jumped up and left halfway through his pitch. He recalls a few executives looking at their watches and tapping on their chairs. When Huggins finished, all eyes turned to Leonard Goldenson, former chairman and president of ABC, to have the first word. Goldenson flatly declared it "the best idea for a TV series I've ever heard." Julius Barnathan, a network executive vice-president, however, called the series concept "the most un-American idea, I've ever heard . . . it's a slap in the face of American justice every week." Barnathan was already worrying about the pile of complaints from viewers, judges, lawyers, and police officers that might flood into the network offices. Huggins defended his ideas, arguing that with all of the courts in the country some of them make mistakes. Another executive wanted to know how the audience would know that the fugitive was innocent. Huggins proposed the idea of an omniscient narrator who would state this fact at the beginning of every episode. Finally, after much deliberation and debate, Goldenson asked Huggins how he wanted to produce the new series. Because Huggins was busy completing a graduate degree at UCLA, he declined to serve as the series' producer but did agree to serve as its creative consultant (Huggins 1998).

Huggins admits that his idea for *The Fugitive* was one that he loved but everyone else hated. In 1960, after he had accepted the position to head up 20th Century Fox's television production department, he had eagerly told Peter Levathes, president of Fox Television, his idea for the series. He recounts the executive's glazed expression and desire to change the subject. Huggins says that Levathes probably thought that he had just "signed up a mad man" as the head of the TV production unit. Despite Levathes' reaction, Huggins insisted that the series' story of an innocent man who has been unjustly convicted and must prove his innocence had an undeniably strong appeal for audiences.

Huggins is one of the few writer-producers who started out in film and ended up working in the television industry. Because the film audience was declining in the 1950s, he thought that television was the best place to be. Huggins began his career as a contract screenwriter for Columbia Pictures penning scripts and story ideas for a variety of film genres, including film noir, comedy, war film, and western. He even directed a successful western, *Hangman's Knot* (1952), starring Randolph Scott and Donna Reed. Huggins's experience as a television producer began in the mid-1950s when he was hired by Warner Brothers to produce ABC's first action-adventure series, *Warner Bros. Presents,* which consisted of three alternating series based on popular Warner theatrical releases: *King's Row*, *Casablanca*, and *Cheyenne*. Following the success of *Cheyenne* (1955–63) as a series, Huggins developed and produced several successful series including *Colt .45* (1957–60), *Maverick* (1957–62), and *77 Sunset Strip* (1958–64). In *Maverick*, he created one of television's first antiheroes, Bret Maverick (James Garner), a con artist/gambler who does not act like the archetypal western hero. If a beautiful woman approaches Maverick to ask for help, he usually tells her how to find the sheriff's office and then avoids her after that. Invariably, despite his best efforts to keep from being involved, he reluctantly solves the dilemmas facing the person or the town (Broughton 1986, 165–66). Huggins injects a sense of humor and fallibility into the traditional stoic western hero and private detective (see, e.g., Stu Bailey in 77 *Sunset Strip*). Huggins was Warner Brothers' most creative and talented producer mainly because he was a writer more than a budget-oriented production supervisor. He established a distinctive vision for each series that he imposed on its main creative team, who shared his perspective and diligently followed it in generating story ideas and in rewriting production scripts (Anderson 1994, 156–90).

Despite Huggins's immense talents, studio head Jack Warner continued to play a peculiar game of "block the royalties" with him. One of Warner's famous edicts was to never give royalty rights to series writers or producers. At Warner Brothers, Huggins never received a "created by" credit for any of the series he created and developed. For example, Warner Brothers bought an unproduced treatment called "The Copper Kings" written by Huggins at Columbia Pictures and asked him to produce *Maverick*'s first episode, "The War of the Silver Kings" (9/22/57), based on it so that they could prevent him from receiving royalty rights to the series. In perhaps the most extreme case, Warner deliberately had the 77 *Sunset Strip* pilot screened for a week in movie theaters in the Caribbean in order to legally establish that the series was derived from a film, rather than short stories and novels written by Huggins. After the 77 *Sunset Strip* incident, Huggins decided to leave Warner Brothers. He became a vice-president in charge of television production at 20th Century Fox Television. For *The Fugitive,* however, Huggins signed a special contract with Quinn Martin Productions and gave them only limited television rights. For himself, he received a "created by" credit, a percentage of the series, and reserved the other rights, such as the one he would exercise to allow the 1993 film to be made. Huggins's deal became known as the "Huggins Contract" because other television writers and producers began demanding similar contracts with the studios and television production companies (Huggins 1998).

The rest of this chapter will explore Huggins's possible sources for the concept of *The Fugitive*. It will also discuss the series' legendary producer, Quinn Martin, the distinctive qualities of a Quinn Martin (Q.M.) Productions TV series, and *The Fugitive*'s place within the Q.M. canon of works. The chapter will also examine the network TV programming and regulatory climate in the 1960s, which laid the groundwork for ABC's creation of *The Fugitive*. The cultural influences on the series will be investigated, including the wanderer-redeemer tradition, semi-anthology series, New Frontier professional dramas, and the longstanding television noir tradition.

Sources for the Series

Where did Huggins obtain the idea for *The Fugitive*? There has been a lot of lively speculation on the possible sources of inspiration for the series. Unfortunately, there are a number of inconsistencies in Huggins's accounts of how he came up with the idea for the series. One obvious source is the famous murder trial of Dr. Samuel Sheppard in 1954, in which the Cleveland osteopath was convicted of murdering his wife. Huggins denies that the Sheppard case served as a model for the series. He says that the reason he made Kimble a doctor was because it was a skill he could use to help people in his travels, although Kimble always has to be careful about using his medical skills because they could reveal his true identity. The Sheppard case, however, was back in the news with Paul Holmes's 1961 best-seller *The Sheppard Murder Case*, which presented the first full-scale reconstruction of the case. Holmes, who covered the original trial, examines the growing public hysteria whipped up against "Dr. Sam," as he became known to millions of headline readers, by the press and how Sheppard was convicted and sentenced for a crime he almost certainly did not commit. In 1964, a federal judge overturned the 1954 verdict and released Sheppard on bail. After examining the court case, the federal judge declared the Sheppard murder trial "a mockery of justice" and chastised the press for serving as "the accuser, judge, and jury" in the case (Cook 1961). In 1966, a new trial acquitted Sheppard of all charges.

Similarities abound between the Sheppard and Kimble murder cases. Each involved a prominent midwestern physician who was accused and convicted of murdering his wife in a highly publicized trial. Both men claimed they saw an unusual-looking suspect unseen by anyone else at the murder scene—Sheppard's "bushy-haired intruder" and Kimble's "one-armed man." Sheppard and Kimble were both convicted on mostly circumstantial evidence. Because Sheppard was the only person proven to be at the murder scene and he had lied earlier about an affair with a beautiful lab technician, it was implied that he was clearly capable of murder. In Kimble's case, evidence of several noisy marital arguments overheard by neighbors provided the jury with all the motivation they needed to convict him. Sheppard and Kimble were both victims of serious flaws within the American justice system.

A lesser-known source for the series is Huggins's experience as a named former member of the Communist Party who had been called before the House Un-American Activities Committee (HUAC) to furnish the names of his socialist comrades. Huggins's guilt over his friendly testimony led him to arrange jobs for his blacklisted friends on several of his less prominent TV series (Buhle and Wagner 2003, 40). He thought HUAC and the Hollywood blacklisting were phony and corrupt exercises. If a film studio head wanted a script written by a blacklisted writer, he could easily have found a way to purchase it

(Huggins 1998). *The Fugitive*'s story of an innocent man falsely accused and convicted solely on incidental evidence and neighborhood gossip serves as an allegory of HUAC and its ruination of scores of careers and lives based only on past associations. Huggins admits that the series' story was probably influenced by the fate of his fellow blacklisted comrades who had to evade the authorities, especially the FBI (Buhle and Wagner 2003, 41). Kimble's situation implicitly speaks to the vulnerability of innocent citizens when the full might of the modern justice system bears down on them.

An often mentioned literary source and inspiration for *The Fugitive* is Victor Hugo's novel *Les Misérables* (1862). Huggins recalls that he sold the series idea to ABC based on a dramatic concept adapted from the classic novel (Buhle and Wagner 2003, 41). The novel features the story of a criminal, Jean Valjean, who is on the lam from a fanatical policeman, Inspector Javert. The British-born, Anglo-Canadian Barry Morse admits that he patterned Gerard on the relentless Javert because of his character's obsessive pursuit of Kimble. I believe that the French name "Gerard" serves as a sly way to associate Morse's relentless character with Javert. As fugitives, Kimble and Valjean both assume aliases and humble jobs to sustain themselves. No matter where the two men go or settle, they cannot escape their criminal past. In *Les Misérables*, the persistent appearance of Javert is a constant reminder of Valjean's criminal history. While Kimble finds human companionship and even romance in his journeys, this solace is always interrupted by the persistent presence of either Gerard or the local police.

One key difference between the two characters is that Valjean is a petty criminal and Kimble has been wrongly convicted of the capital crime of murder. Both the novel and the TV series question the fairness of the justice system. Valjean ends up in prison for stealing a loaf of bread to feed his starving family. Kimble is wrongly convicted based on slim evidence and local gossip. Kathryn Grossman states that the central theme of

Les Misérables is the poetics of aesthetic, spiritual, and political transcendence through the act of self-sacrifice for a better world (1994, 4–8). The novel is filled with moments of moral and ethical conversions. For instance, Valjean is spiritually redeemed when a kindly bishop not only lies to protect him from the law for stealing two silver candlesticks but then gives them to him. The bishop's act of grace is reproduced several times in Valjean's life: he confesses his identity in court to save a man arrested as Jean Valjean, and he sets the policeman Javert free from being executed by revolutionaries. Kimble also performs acts of self-sacrifice to redeem troubled children and adults. In the episode "Cry Uncle" (12/1/64), Kimble risks his own capture by police to prove to an orphaned boy that someone does care about him. The boy decides in light of Kimble's selfless act to stay at the orphanage and fight the county board's efforts to send him to the state mental hospital. Kimble's self-sacrificial acts serve as transcendent moments of sublime idealism that resonate well beyond their dramatic contexts. The main theme of *The Fugitive* can thus be seen as mid-twentieth-century secular humanism opposed to institutional bureaucracy. Gerard, an inflexible police detective, represents the impersonal, authoritarian side of modern bureaucracies.

Another possible literary source for the series is David Goodis's 1946 novel *Dark Passage*, which was later adapted by Warner Brothers into the 1947 film noir classic of the same name starring Humphrey Bogart and Lauren Bacall. In the novel, a fugitive, Vincent Parry, who was wrongly convicted of killing his wife, escapes from prison to search for the real murderer. However, because Parry is too well-known, he is forced to seek a new face from a plastic surgeon. Parry and Kimble are both ordinary, middle-class citizens who are assisted by the common people they meet in their journeys who sympathize with them. Parry is described as a man who is not especially aggressive or physically powerful, but he is equal to the occasion when threatened by violence. Kimble has a similar demeanor and physical presence. The escape of both men is merely a prologue for ensuing events involving their plight as desperate, hunted men who must keep running and hiding while at the same time searching for the means to prove their innocence (Finestone 2009). Ursini argues that Parry and Kimble convey the frightened look and mannerisms of a hunted animal (1996, 284). Goodis describes Parry's initial reactions to Irene, the woman who would help him: "She saw him. She beckoned to him. There was authority in the beckoning and Parry was frightened. He completed the turn and he started to run" (1999, 20). Kimble's nervous, darting eyes, constant melancholy expression, and stooped posture all express the signs of a man who is always aware that he is being hunted and therefore must never let his guard down.

The similarities between the novel and the series led the Goodis estate to sue United Artist Television for copyright infringement. The lawsuit, which became entangled in a complex copyright status legal argument, was finally settled in 1972 for only $12,000 awarded to the Goodis estate when their lawyers admitted that the serialized novel had entered into the public domain and that Warner Brothers had legally obtained the rights to produce the series.

A Q.M. Production

The Fugitive is also best remembered for its association with television producer Quinn Martin. Most television viewers in the 1960s and 1970s could easily identify Q.M. series because they were always introduced by a booming, offscreen male voice, featured overly dramatic episode titles, and contained identifiable segmented dramatic acts. Q.M. Productions' first series, *The New Breed* (1961–62), a police drama, is unusual in that it was unsuccessful. *The Fugitive* became Q.M.'s second series. Huggins worked with Martin on planning the series' pilot episode, "Fear in a Desert City" (9/17/63). Huggins confesses that he had to disabuse Martin of a few of his odd series ideas, including having the fugitive keep his same name everywhere he goes, instead of using an alias, and maintaining a pocket diary to record his thoughts. Huggins argued that every time the police would stop Kimble, they would find the diary and instantly know he was a wanted murderer. It is true that the series' serious, melodramatic tone is typical of most Q.M. productions. *The Fugitive* does not feature any of Huggins's recognizable self-effacing, antihero characters or display any satirical humor. However, Huggins admits that Martin did an excellent job of producing and maintaining consistent quality throughout the series (Huggins 1998).

Before producing the series, Martin served as executive producer on the highly rated ABC police drama *The Untouchables* (1959–63). Each episode of *The Untouchables* was framed by the "historically authoritative" voice of Walter Winchell, the well-known newspaper gossip columnist. This narrative framing device, coupled with the representation of historical figures (Eliot Ness, Frank Nitti), gave the series the texture of a TV docudrama. Another Martin innovation was to focus on the long-term tensions building up between the plainly dressed, laconic Eliot Ness (Robert Stack) and the gaudily dressed, loud-mouthed Frank Nitti (Bruce Gordon), which dramatically overshadowed the story particulars in any episode. This narrative technique of highlighting and sustaining the psychological battle between cop and criminal across episodes would later appear in such police drama series as Stephen J. Cannell's *Wiseguy* (1987–90) and Michael Mann's *Crime Story* (1986–88). Martin himself would cultivate another long-term tense relationship between cop and criminal in his next series, *The Fugitive*. The dramatic twist is that the criminal is not really a criminal after all. After *The Fugitive*, Martin became one of television's most prolific and successful producers, overseeing a wide range of hour-long dramatic series, including *Twelve O'Clock High* (1964–67), *The F.B.I.* (1965–74), *Cannon* (1971–76), *The Streets of San Francisco* (1972–77), and *Barnaby Jones* (1973–80).

In 1962 Martin, who had been a film editor at Universal when David Janssen was a contract player there, asked the actor to star in a TV series he was planning to produce. At the time, Janssen was starring as the lead in *Richard Diamond, Private Detective* (1957–60), a series that most critics considered average in terms of stories, characters, and performances. In his next series, however, Janssen cast as Kimble would begin "to develop a whole range of facial gestures and vocal inflections that had a distinctive impact on the small screen" (Thorburn 1977, 192). It is Janssen's performance as Kimble that resonates well beyond the series' stories and that moves even the most action-oriented episodes into moments of strong emotional intimacy. Janssen is adept at employing the nuances of gesture, vocal inflection, and movement to suggest Kimble's humane but anxious character. Janssen is accomplished in the type of subtle performance that characterized the best of television melodrama. John O'Connor (1980) asserts that Janssen consistently gave a compelling, emotional performance that seemed to surpass any possible weaknesses in the television script. O'Connor places Janssen in the company of a limited number of TV actors, such as Robert Conrad, Raymond Burr, James Garner, and Robert Vaughn, who learned the "minimal-histrionic demands" of television and who have the type of quiet, forceful presence that can transcend itself through the small screen.

Martin's casting of Janssen is an example of his tight control of the series. He is notable for his paternalistic approach to television production. At Q.M. Productions, writers, directors, producers, and production managers were assigned and stayed within their specific roles. Martin is often compared with film studio heads like Warner and L. B. Mayer because he oversees and completely controls the creative content of all of his series.

Not only does this control extend to approving each story idea, but it also involves working to create a consistent viewpoint in terms of story, visual style, and casting for each series. Once these elements are firmly established, he then grants considerable freedom to his creative staff (Newcomb and Alley 1983, 57–60). Q.M. producer Alan Armer credits Martin with maintaining visual realism and authenticity with his TV series by incorporating more on-location and night-for-night shooting as he did in *The Fugitive*. Armer says that, at the time, most producers would simply darken film footage during the day to simulate nighttime to save money (quoted in Cooper 1997).

The series' first episode features an unusual (at least for episodic television) handheld shot following a cocktail waitress as she walks up to Kimble, who is busy tending bar. The shot captures and expresses the hustle and bustle of the bar. Although *The Fugitive* follows the standard rear-screen projection method for filming interior shots between actors in a moving automobile, several episodes are notable for incorporating uncommon subjective shots through the vehicle windshield. In the episode "Devil's Carnival" (12/22/64) the viewer is given a subjective viewpoint through the windshield of a truck as it approaches and evades a police roadblock. Through the windshield, the viewer experiences the truck almost hitting a pedestrian, who is saved by Kimble's wrestling the steering wheel away from the driver. These subjective shots heighten the dramatic tension of the scenes as the audience can empathize with Kimble's fears of the roadblock and in the possible horrible sight of an innocent bystander being hit by the truck. Despite the limited budgets of episodic television production, Martin strived to emulate feature film quality and control as much as he could. Armer asserts that Martin would often roll a percentage of his production company's income back into his series' productions so as to maintain their consistent production quality (quoted in Cooper 1997).

Several of Martin's works, especially *The F.B.I.* and *The Untouchables*, have received harsh criticism as being prime examples of television's tacit support of political and social repression mainly because of their stern upholding of the status quo and implicit endorsement of conservative ideals. Martin admits that many of his series tend to idealize traditional law-and-order authority figures like police officers and federal agents. Horace Newcomb and Robert Alley (1983), however, contend that the central thrust of a Q.M. series is not political ideology but human emotion and pathos. Each Q.M. series strives to create believable characters from most facets of the political spectrum, characters who elicit a wide range of emotions including victimization, frustration, and even anger at the social system. Even in his more traditional crime dramas, like *The F.B.I.*, the stories are more centered on understanding the psychological motivations of the criminals than celebrating the hard-working federal agents. *The Fugitive* is the Q.M. series with the strongest sense of humanity and moral ambiguity, where justice and the legal system are repeatedly questioned (Newcomb and Alley 1983, 47–56). Throughout the series, Gerard, as a confirmed believer in and enforcer of the system, continuously runs into Kimble's indelible humanity. Every week as Kimble is pursued by the indefatigable machinery of American law enforcement, *The Fugitive* brings an ironic twist to the ideal that American justice is blind to all who come before her.

TV Programming and Cultural Influences

From 1961 to 1962, the television industry underwent a full-on assault by federal regulators. *The Fugitive* was developed and produced within this highly charged regulatory climate. FCC chairman Newton Minow launched the first assault in his infamous 1961 speech to a roomful of network broadcasters. Minow referred to network television as a "vast wasteland" and berated the mayhem and violence in programming. He also bemoaned the oversaturation of westerns on television and rebuked them for sending the wrong cold war message about American culture: "What will the people of other countries think of us when they see our western bad men and good men punching each other in the jaw in between the shooting?" (Minow 1961). In the 1958–59 television season, there were twenty-eight prime-time westerns on the network schedules.

The second assault came in the summer of 1961 and January 1962 when the Senate Subcommittee to Investigate Juvenile Delinquency investigated the supposed connection between television violence and juvenile crime. The committee was commonly called the Dodd hearings after its colorful chairman, Thomas Dodd. The Dodd hearings targeted several shows for excessive violence, including ABC's prime-time series *The Untouchables*, *Cheyenne*, and a notorious episode from the dramatic anthology series *Bus Stop* (1961–62).[2] A year later, Huggins, who produced *Cheyenne* and *Bus Stop*, wrote a scathing rebuttal to Minow's speech defending the artistic merits of popular entertainment while labeling the chairman's criticism of television as elitist.

Goldenson at ABC responded to the change in the regulatory climate by naming Tom Moore its new president. Moore declared that one of ABC's past problems was its lack of program development and that for the 1963–64 television season it would spend nearly $3 million in that area. He promised that about 60 percent of the prime-time schedule would consist of new series. Despite the tremendous popularity of ABC's action-adventure programming in the mid- to late 1950s, the network's ratings began to decline in the 1961–62 television season partly because of the excess of westerns and other action-adventure programming on all three networks. ABC wanted to create kinder, gentler dramatic programming that did not rely solely on physical violence and murder to attract adult audiences. Goldenson, in search of new programming, approached many of his previously successful producers, including Roy Huggins.

Wanderer-Redeemer Tradition

With *The Fugitive*, ABC turned to producing a type of dramatic programming I call the contemporary, nonviolent wanderer-redeemer series. The nonviolent wanderer-redeemer differs from the traditional violent wanderer-redeemer in that he does not resolve social problems through the cleansing act of violence but through selfless acts of compassion and kindness. Robert Jewett and John Shelton Lawrence assert that the violent redeemer who redeems society through ritualized violence and the nonviolent redeemer who redeems society through love and compassion are both examples of the mono-mythic, Judeo-Christian redeemer figure that has come to dominate western popular culture (1977, 195–96).

The television western cowboy is a perfect example of the violent redeemer figure. The cowboy has a special talent: he can shoot straighter and faster than other men and has an innate sense of justice. These characteristics, however, make it impossible for him to fully assimilate into society. His destiny is to defend society and to eradicate evil through the act of ritual combat (Jewett and Lawrence 1977, 195–96). In *Cheyenne*, Cheyenne Bodie (Clint Walker), a former frontier scout, is a lone redeemer who wanders from one frontier community to another, inserting himself into a series of local situations filled with conflict, and then handily resolving them through either deadly gunplay or physical violence. However, the chivalrous, "educated, knight-errant gunslinger" Paladin (Richard Boone) on CBS's *Have Gun Will Travel* (1957–63) prefers to base himself in a swank San Francisco hotel suite. Once he receives a payment from a client, he willingly takes on a specific mission of justice or mercy. The urbane gunfighter named himself Paladin after the legendary officers of Charlemagne's medieval court. The series' identifying graphic was Paladin's calling card bearing an image of a white knight chess piece and the inscription, "Have Gun, Will Travel . . . Wire Paladin, San Francisco"

(Orlick). Through its allusions, *Have Gun Will Travel* self-consciously acknowledges Paladin's mythic role as a violent redeemer.

Christopher Anderson states that Huggins in *The Fugitive* "wanted to update the western by placing its wandering hero in a contemporary setting. In transposing the stock figure of the wanderer from the mythic landscape of the West to the landscape of 1960s America, he created a new and unsettling dramatic hero for television, a rootless, paranoid loner, the most unsettled character on the New Frontier of Kennedy-era America" (1997). Kimble's solitary status allows him to travel crosscountry, enter into new communities, and encounter a diversity of social types. Invariably, he comes to the aid of the socially powerless, especially women and children. But unlike the gunslinging western hero, Kimble resolves conflicts through selfless acts of compassion and kindness rather than through violent combat. Kimble represents the merger between the television male redeemer figure and the wanderer hero in American and European literature who leaves society, more or less alone, in order to achieve a heightened level of moral awareness in the wilderness, at sea, or on the margins of settled society. The literary male wanderer hero thematic dates from Homer's *The Odyssey* and encompasses such seemingly disparate works as James Fenimore Cooper's *The Deerslayer* and Herman Melville's *Moby Dick*. Unlike the violent western wanderer-redeemer who is situated in the historical past, the nonviolent wanderer-redeemer is a contemporary protagonist. The television wanderer-redeemer's journey is a redemptive one; he takes to the road to escape a troubled past in search of salvation and a new life.

The earliest examples of the contemporary television nonviolent social redeemer are Buz (George Maharis) and Tod (Martin Milner) in the CBS series *Route 66*, which ran from 1960 to 1964 on CBS. Buz and Tod are somewhat clean-cut, sanitized versions of Kerouac's Beat characters Sal and Dean in his novel *On the Road* (1957). Tod is the Yale-educated, introspective character, whose family's wealth disappeared with the death of his father, and his buddy Buz is a tough, streetwise, impulsive guy from Hell's Kitchen. The two cruise across the American countryside in a sleek, shiny Corvette, which serves as the series' primary symbol of freedom and as such it is a symbol most accessible to middle-class suburbanites (Newcomb 1974, 141–43). Whether they would admit it or not, Buz and Tod took to the road on an existential search for meaning in their lives. Although Kimble is a fugitive, his cross-country journeys are also an implicit quest for new social encounters and experiences. Hal Himmelstein argues that as the western and police/detective genres began to wane in the early 1960s, a new genre began to emerge based on traveling across America's landscape. He asserts that this romantic motif came to dominate television melodramas in this period. Himmelstein contends that the twin postwar developments of the suburbs and the increased dependence on automobiles and superhighways led to America's renewed preoccupation with speed and travel (1984, 171–74).

In *Route 66*, Buz and Tod function as "unofficial social workers and psychoanalysts" who frequently assist characters caught up in emotional crises (Alvey 1997, 153). Kimble assumes a similar "knight-errant" role in *The Fugitive*. Because he is constantly being hunted for a crime he did not commit, guilt-ridden over the death of his wife, and unable to relax and settle down, Kimble evokes strong empathy and identification with male and female audiences. Kimble exemplifies Ien Ang's "melodramatic identification" because his long-suffering, tortured character captures the hearts of both men and women (1996, 72–80). *The Fugitive* shares characteristics with television family melodramas in that its narratives highlight the meaningfulness of ordinary suffering and the significance of close relationships, especially familial ones (O'Donnell 2007, 123). Melodramas are especially adept at depicting characters as victims of social conformity and psychological neuroses. Because melodramas focus on revealing the social and power relations that underlie everyday life, they address contemporary social issues and concerns (Schatz 1991, 149–52). Peter Brooks (1976) argues that melodrama intensifies and externalizes its emotions. A character's emotional life is mapped onto objects and places, and is "mirrored back to them through other characters" they encounter and through his or her gestures and body movement (Schmidt 2010). In a melodramatic sense, all of the disaffected, socially trapped characters whom Kimble helps are emotional expressions of his tormented inner state. The beautiful women Kimble meets and often romances are variations on his late wife. Each child he meets and befriends represents the child he and Helen never had. Each *Fugitive* episode creates a moral universe that reflects and expresses his moral dilemma. Rugolo's musical score accentuates the rise and fall and shifting of dramatic emotions in the episodes. Kimble, in helping these troubled characters find a stable selfhood, provides audiences with a satisfying dramatic escape and release from the numbing routines and ambiguous realities of everyday life.

Marc Eliot suggests that Kimble's official designation as a fugitive brings him a new sense of liberation. He argues that Kimble's previous suburban life was essentially unhappy and unfulfilled, while his new one stands as testimony to the value of human freedom (1981, 46–49). It is true that in the episode "The Girl from Little Egypt" (12/24/63), the pre-fugitive Kimble with his prematurely gray hair appears older than the fugitive Kimble. While Kimble's status does provide him with a stronger sense of freedom from social commitments than his former life did, it is also an experience tempered by constant fear and paranoia.

Robert Alvey, who has labeled *Route 66* television's "seminal road series," argues that the road itself serves as a multivalent cultural symbol for each era and generation of American life. For the Beats, the road serves as a revitalized source of freedom as well as an avenue to intersect with the nation's marginalized minorities, especially Native Americans and African Americans.

Richard Kimble (Janssen), working as a sail tester, enjoys the freedom of the open sea in the 1963 episode "Never Wave Goodbye, Part 1."

The Beats wanted to reclaim the American road as a new symbol of freedom away from the impoverished images associated with the Great Depression. For *Route 66*, which arrived with Kennedy and the New Frontier, the road serves as a bridge between the disquiet and conformity of the 1950s and the restless, optimistic spirit of the early 1960s (1997, 151–52). For *The Fugitive*, coming in the wake of the New Frontier and at the beginning of the turbulent 1960s, the road symbolizes the dark side of the American dream whereby a law-abiding, professional suddenly finds himself systematically hunted down.

Semi-Anthology Series

ABC also turned to producing more so-called semi-anthology series. Semi-anthology series have a small set of continuing characters whom viewers readily recognize coupled with changing weekly dramatic scenarios featuring well-known television actors. These series fused the best elements of the dramatic anthology series (e.g., *Kraft Television Theatre* [1947–58], *Playhouse 90* [1956–61]) with those of the episodic series. *The Fugitive* follows the conventional narrative and dramatic structure of a semi-anthology series. ABC's *Wagon Train* (1957–65) and *Naked City* (1958–63) are generally considered the founding examples of the semi-anthology series. *Wagon Train* established the narrative premise of the road as perfectly suited for the semi-anthology format. *Wagon Train*'s regular set of characters and their steady westward movement provided viewers with an accessible narrative frame for the presentation of weekly episodic character studies built around "guest stars" they would meet along the trail. The appearance and promotion of guest stars became a stable commercial element in television dramas in the 1960s (Alvey 1997, 143–44).

Despite a few early successes, most semi-anthology series were plagued by weak continuing characters that were tangential to the guest characters and episode narratives. These series also featured unnatural settings and dramatic scenarios. ABC's short-lived series *Bus Stop* is one example. The bus stop in the series is a diner in Sunshine, Colorado. Continuing characters included the diner owner, a waitress, the local sheriff, and the district attorney. The series features stories of people passing through the small town via its interstate bus service. Huggins, who produced the series based on the William Inge play of the same name, admitted that the series' dramatic premise was weak and contrived (1998). *The Fugitive* avoids these dramatic pitfalls by offering its viewers a strong set of continuing characters for viewer identification and interest including Kimble, Gerard, and Fred Johnson (Bill Raisch), who were central to the series' stories. Kimble, in particular, is in every episode. Secondary continuing characters include Donna (Jacqueline Scott) and Leonard Taft (Richard Anderson, Lin McCarthy), Kimble's sister and brother-in-law. These characters gave the program a serialized sense of its own continuous history and kept its central story in a steady state of narrative progression. The series' premise that Kimble must stay one step ahead of his pursuers while following the one-armed man led to a host of new settings and places every week. He also needed to sustain himself through various odd jobs, which presented him with yet more opportunities to meet a wide range of people. David Marc and Robert Thompson argue that Martin is "sentimental, even romantic, about the values of the American working class" in the series (1992, 155). Despite Kimble's close relationships with working-class people and his image as a hard worker, the series does not hide the fact that part of his punishment is his inability to practice his chosen middle-class profession. In the episode "May God Have Mercy" (3/16/65), for example, Kimble's lowly status is emphasized by the fact that he now works as a hospital orderly in the same institution where he once served as a physician.

The series' narrative formula of having Kimble encounter and help troubled people provides the perfect framework for intensely dramatic character explorations within the confines of a weekly chase drama. Some of *The Fugitive*'s best-known guest stars include Charles Bronson, Bruce Dern, Angie Dickinson, Ossie Davis, Robert Duvall, Ron Howard, Mickey Rooney,

Kurt Russell, Telly Savalas, Tuesday Weld, and Jack Weston. The series' producers relied on the guest actors' public star images in casting them in the episodes. These star images were composites of the actors' film, television, and stage roles combined with their public and private lives. For instance, in the episode "This'll Kill You" (1/18/66), Mickey Rooney is cast as a doomed ex-bookie with a mob contract on his head. In the late 1950s and early 1960s, Rooney played a series of urban low-life characters, including the corrupt union boss in *The Big Operator* (1959), the boxing cut-man in *Requiem for a Heavyweight* (1962), and the crooked horse jockey in *The Twilight Zone* episode "The Last Night of a Jockey" (10/25/63). Tuesday Weld was cast as a dangerously manipulative sculptress in the series' episode "Dark Corner" (11/10/64). At the time, Weld was known as one of Hollywood's bad girls, partly because of her well-known TV role as the beautiful, scheming, money-hungry teenager Thalia Menninger on the sitcom *The Many Loves of Dobie Gillis* (1959–63). Weld also had a reputation for having affairs with famous older men such as Elvis Presley.

New Frontier Professional Dramas

ABC and the other networks continued to produce the so-called New Frontier professional dramas in the early 1960s. Mary Ann Watson asserts that these series were based on "liberal social themes in which the protagonists were professionals in service to society." She maintains that the young characters in these series shared a strong sentiment for social change and set out to create a better, fairer America one week at a time (1990, 43–72). ABC's professional dramas included *Ben Casey* (1961–66), a medical drama, *The Breaking Point* (1963–64), a psychiatric drama, and *Channing* (1963–64), a series set on a college campus. These programs emerged partly because of a successful programming cycle, which began with series like *The Defenders* and *Dr. Kildare* (1961–66), and they were marketed

Tuesday Weld as the blind Mattie Braydon with Kimble in the 1964 episode "Dark Corner."

as the networks' attempt to produce more socially relevant programming.

The Fugitive shares some similarities with the New Frontier professional dramas. Kimble certainly assists people who are socially powerless or marginalized by society. Like the professionals, Kimble resolves individual problems using compassion and reason. He also shares with the professionals an inherent disillusionment with inflexible, parochial values. In the episode "The Witch" (9/24/63), for example, Kimble battles small-town provincialism to help an unmarried female schoolteacher retain her teaching post in the face of unwarranted rumors about her past that continue to tarnish her reputation. Also, just as Kimble's past as a convicted murderer keeps invading his present existence, many of the characters he meets are constantly haunted or punished by their own pasts.

The Fugitive was also part of what Watson refers to as the 1963–64 "Civil Rights TV Season" in which many series featured African Americans as regular characters. Throughout its run, the series cast well-known African American actors in professional roles, including Ossie Davis as a police detective, Ivan Dixon as a neuropsychiatrist, and Percy Rodriguez as a deputy sheriff. In the episode "Decision in the Ring" (10/22/63), Kimble takes the job of a cut-man for a black boxer, but his medical knowledge arouses suspicion. Kimble convinces the boxer, a medical school drop-out, to give up his life-threatening boxing career to pursue a career in medicine. The episode also features a party in which blacks and whites mix socially. Although *The Fugitive* did not directly confront or address the issue of racial equality, it did contribute to the public acceptance of African Americans in prime-time television.

However, unlike the young, idealistic professionals in New Frontier dramas, Kimble is a fallen professional turned criminal on the run. He is unable to serve as a physician and must sustain himself through unskilled jobs. Although the New Frontier characters work within the system to change it, the fugitive not only is "outside" the system but has been condemned to death by it. Also, although the series reveals the inherent flaws in the American justice system, it does not suggest any workable solutions for fixing it. In fact, beyond Kimble's hope of finding the one-armed man and overturning his conviction, the series offers a rather bleak outlook in this period of liberal social reform.

TV Noir

Huggins admitted that *The Fugitive*'s story of an innocent man on the run searching for evidence to prove his innocence was certainly not a new one. It is a common theme in many Hollywood noir films from the 1930s, 1940s, and 1950s, including *You Only Live Once* (1937), *They Live by Night* (1949), *Dark Passage* (1947), and *The Wrong Man* (1956). They all feature stories of sympathetic and tragic characters on the lam from the law. Kimble, who is surely an empathetic character for audiences, follows a TV noir tradition of the innocent man who keeps running in order to survive and to find a way to redeem himself. James Ursini writes that *The Fugitive* is "the most self-conscious *noir* series" and certainly the most successful one on American television (1996, 284). He asserts that noir themes and style have influenced television, especially in the 1950s and 1960s in what might be called television's "classic period" of noir with its black-and-white programming. The earliest appearance of the noir style on television was the series *China Smith* (1952–54). The series starred Dan Duryea as a crafty con artist and sometime private detective who operated out of a bar in Singapore and traveled throughout the Far East for adventure and profit. *China Smith* established several television noir conventions, including the appearance of rain-soaked city streets, low-key lighting patterns, hard-boiled dialogue, first-person narration, and a main character who follows his own sense of justice. *China Smith* was followed by other noir-style episodic series including *Dante* (1960–61), *Mickey Spillane's Mike Hammer* (1958–59), *The Man with a Camera* (1958–60), *Richard Diamond, Private Detective* (1957–60), *Peter Gunn* (1958–61), and *Johnny Staccato* (1959–60).

At the heart of *The Fugitive* is noir's core theme of the existential search for self and identity in a morally ambiguous and irrational world. This theme is usually represented in the story of a social outcast or outsider (Glover and Bushman 2006, 70). Most often the outsider figure is a victim of fate, a person who finds his life suddenly turned upside down, becomes alienated from friends, associates, and family, and finds himself in mortal danger. Although noir's estranged protagonists have been detectives, ex-convicts, drifters, musicians, and lower-level business executives, Kimble's character represents the social pinnacle of middle-class professionalism—a medical doctor. Kimble is also television's most powerful representation of fatalistic alienation. Deprived of his social identity and profession, he is filled with guilt over the death of his wife and his inability to save her. He is also constantly pursued by the relentless Gerard. Kimble is in a constant state of heightened anxiety and fear. Huggins, in his original pitch to ABC, succinctly summarized the core themes of the series: "Kimble's life as a fugitive will relate to deep and responsive drives . . . not the least of which is that Kimble lives with alienation and anxiety." The series' opening title sequence economically establishes a dark mood of fatalistic alienation, which would influence its four-year run on television (Ursini 1996, 284). The opening image of a train transporting Kimble to be executed is a familiar noir motif (e.g., *Double Indemnity* [1944], *Human Desire* [1954]) that serves as a visual analogue for the character's doomed fate. In turn, the train derailment serves as a visual representation of fate intervening in Kimble's life and the beginning of his long hunt for justice.

The Fugitive stands as a television critique of the American cold war compulsion to snoop on one's neighbors by having its main protagonist (Kimble) become the unwitting victim of nosy neighbors: Kimble's conviction rests partly on the hearsay of his neighbors. Noir's postwar paranoia is evident in such explicitly anti-Communist films as *I Was a Communist for the F.B.I.* (1951), *My Son John* (1952), and *Walk East on Beacon* (1952). These films seemed to implicitly legitimize and sanction the cold war notion of spying on one's neighbors and even family members to protect the American home front (Spicer 2002, 69). There were a few films, like Alfred Hitchcock's *Rear Window* (1954), which did critique America's postwar obsession with spying on one's neighbors by having the voyeur become the victim-object of his obsessive voyeurism. *The Fugitive* argues that the same cold war cultural obsessions and law enforcement mechanisms employed to detect internal "enemies" in American society can just as easily be used against its own citizenry. The series taps into a cultural paranoia not about an internal, subversive enemy but about the culture's incessant voyeuristic obsessions with "the private" and fear of government's growing institutional powers turned against an innocent citizen.

Stylistically, *The Fugitive* features several devices common to noir. For instance, while most of the series' stories follow the traditional chronological structure of exposition to resolution, a few episodes have a complex chronological order, which is a common noir technique for expressing character feelings of "hopelessness and lost time" (Schrader 1996, 58). In "The Girl from Little Egypt" (12/24/63), for example, the story uses a series of flashbacks to provide viewers with a glimpse into Kimble's unhappy marriage as well as the events that led up to his wife's murder. These flashbacks also give us a sense of Kimble's guilt-ridden conscience in his sweating and constant tossing and turning in his hospital bed. Other noir stylistics in *The Fugitive* include Conrad's hard-boiled voiceover narration; tough-sounding episode titles, such as "Everybody Gets Hit in the Mouth Sometime" (3/9/1965), "Escape into Black" (11/17/64), and "Detour on a Road Going Nowhere" (12/8/64); night-for-night and on-location black-and-white photography; and familiar noir locations (e.g., bars, pool halls, train stations, wet city streets, dark roads). Quinn Martin "was very conscious of the extent to which black-and-white photography, that sort of shadowed effect that was created by these dark streets, was an explicit echo of film noir," and the producer saw the series as a way "to recapture some of the ambience of film noir" (Robertson 1993, 21). In the early 1960s, distinct noir stylistics would have been both familiar to and slightly nostalgic for television audiences.

The Fugitive's pilot episode, "Fear in a Desert City," illustrates the incorporation of noir stylistics and establishes the series' familiar story formula. The episode's title asserts that noir paranoia is present in the American Southwest. Kimble arrives at a community (in this case, Tucson, Arizona) and befriends a woman in jeopardy (a piano player, Monica Welles [Vera Miles]). As with most *Fugitive* episodes, the exteriors are shot on location to express a strong sense of geographic verisimilitude with audiences. Kimble, working as a bartender, protects Monica when she is bothered by a male patron at the bar. He later learns that the patron is Ed Welles (Brian Keith), her jealous, drunken husband who employs his wealth and influence to threaten Kimble with the local police. Kimble later confesses to Monica his story and thereby informs viewers about why he is on the run. Because of his protective, decent behavior, Monica accepts his innocence and he is able to escape the town before the authorities close in on his location. Kimble's quiet demeanor and empathetic character assure viewers that his ongoing plight will be worth following.

In the noir world, nighttime represents fear, paranoia, and danger for the protagonist. It is at night that the dark forces, which are kept at bay during the bright daylight, come to the forefront. The series' night-for-night photography frequently places Kimble against a black sky or near a dark space that threatens to engulf him. The dark areas characteristic of noir's low-key lighting serve to mask a character's hidden motivations, mysteries, or past. For Ed Welles, the darkness represents his jealous and violent temperament. For Kimble, this darkness embodies his guilt over his wife's death, his murder conviction, and his fear of being caught and executed for a crime he didn't commit. Nighttime has a special meaning for Kimble and

Monica Welles (Vera Miles) on piano, Jim Lincoln (Janssen) tending bar, and Edward Welles (Brian Keith) as customer in the series' 1963 pilot episode "Fear in a Desert City."

his predicament. Kimble and his wife fought at night, a fight that ended with her death. It was at night that fate intervened, causing the train to derail and freeing him to pursue his long, dangerous journey for justice. In this first episode, the story is structured so that Kimble faces his most dramatically perilous moments at night: he rescues Monica from her physically abusive husband in the bar parking lot, he is picked up and interrogated by the local police after leaving the bar, and he fights a gun-toting Ed who tries to stop Monica, her son Mark, and Kimble from boarding a bus to leave Tucson. While *The Fugitive* does not rigidly follow this narrative model of placing its most dramatic scenes at night, it is a recurring noir pattern in the series. At the end of the episode, the final shots show Kimble walking away from the bus depot into the dark night and then alongside a set of railroad tracks, which serve as a visual and symbolic reminder that his journey began with the fateful train derailment. The image of Kimble walking alone against the black night sky accentuates his loneliness and his inability to escape his dark past.

This episode, as with most of the series' episodes, follows the standard Hollywood continuity style developed and propagated in the studio telefilm productions of the late 1950s. Each shot, camera movement, and edit choice is motivated by the dramatic context of the story and its characters. For instance, in a scene between Kimble and Monica in her apartment, camera movement is motivated by Monica and Kimble's physical actions of walking over to the kitchen to pour themselves another cup of coffee from a coffee pot. Despite the conventional nature of most of the episode's scenes, certain dramatic moments are punctuated by distinctive stylistic features. When Ed confronts Kimble, Monica, and Mark at the bus depot, the scene is shot from a low-angle position to emphasize Ed's physically threatening presence and to present an unstable situation. A common noir feature is the use of an unsettling and disorienting mise-en-scène to represent the protagonist or a character's unstable mental state. In many ways, *The Fugitive* marked the end of the classic period of TV noir. The series' final season (1966–67) brought a shift away from its noir-like, black-and-white photography to color and, thereby, a termination of many of its stylistic features. These noir features gave *The Fugitive* a dark, existential tone that added a layer of mythic and emotional resonance to its stories and characters.

The Fugitive was the product of both a highly charged broadcast regulatory environment in the early 1960s and the fertile, creative mind of Roy Huggins. It was also the first successful dramatic series produced by the legendary Q.M. Productions. The series' story of an innocent man falsely accused and convicted on the lam from the law resonates deeply with postwar existentialism, cold war paranoia, and McCarthyism.

The contemporary and timeless story of a man who must take to the road in search of moral and spiritual redemption firmly places it within the camp of the western literary and mythic wanderer-redeemer tradition. For Kimble, the road serves as both a liberating force from the stifling conformity of his former suburban, middle-class life and a never-ending, nihilistic nightmare filled with fear, paranoia, and dread. This inherent contradiction between freedom and fatalism lies at the heart of the series, making it one of the most captivating series on television. *The Fugitive* was popular with adult audiences because its characters and stories intersected with cultural and social debates taking place in 1960s America. Chapter 3 will examine and delve into the dominant social themes represented in and across episodes of the long-running series.

Chapter 3
A Thematic Analysis of *The Fugitive*

The Fugitive was popular with audiences in the 1960s because its characters and stories connected with ongoing cultural struggles over individual freedom and social justice. These struggles, which had various degrees of intensity, included African Americans, whites, Latino Americans, Native Americans, college students and disaffected intellectuals, young people, women, and the poor. Early signs of this conflict could be seen in the 1950s with the work of cultural rebels such as the Beat writers Jack Kerouac and Allen Ginsberg, rebellious actors like Marlon Brando and James Dean, and rock 'n' roll singers like Elvis Presley and Chuck Berry, as well as the participation of blacks in civil rights protests in the South (Clecak 1983, 16–17).[3]

In his travels, Kimble meets and befriends alienated individuals and helps them overcome social, cultural, and psychological barriers to freedom and self-expression. Kimble is television's first true victim-hero, an innocent, hunted man who systematically has more in common with the each episode's estranged characters than with its assorted villains or authority figures. In turn, the people Kimble meets tend to sympathize with him because they themselves are social outsiders. These people are "Americans marginalized by society, not because of what they have allegedly done but because of who they are" (Zane 2007). In order to delve into the relationship between the series and these cultural struggles, this chapter will examine the following dominant themes represented in the episodes: individualism, love and marriage, the culture of professionalism, modern science and technology, and social justice and authority.

Individualism

In American society, there is a tension between the capitalist economy and the political state, and the freedoms granted to individuals. During World War II and the economic growth of the early 1950s, individuals were expected to defer gratification and sacrifice for results that would come later in life. However, in the peace and affluence of the late 1950s and early 1960s, individual expectations—material, psychological, and spiritual—increased and soared to new heights (Clecak 1983, 111–12). In turn, postwar institutional bureaucracies sought to moderate these expectations by inscribing people into specific social roles. By the 1960s, several social observers were concerned about the loss of individual freedom in the face of the increased role of centralized government, large corporations, and mass media in America's growing society. Although social critics such as David Reisman, William Whyte, and C. Wright Mills had expressed similar worries in the 1950s, the accelerated pace of science and technology brought a new urgency to the public debate concerning the pressures of social conformity on the individual.

During the 1964 presidential campaign, Senator Barry Goldwater (R-AZ) used the perceived loss of individual freedom as one of his primary campaign themes. As President Lyndon Johnson expanded the federal government's role in civil rights and anti-poverty legislation, Goldwater believed big government was the main threat to individual freedom. In his first campaign speech, Goldwater spoke on this issue.

> The individual, the private man, the whole man—you!—Today, stands in danger of becoming the forgotten man of our collectivized complex times. . . . Responsibility has shifted from the family to the bureaucrat, from the neighborhood to the arbitrary and distant agency. Goals are set, roles are assigned, promises are made—all by the remote control of central government. (1965)

The emerging New Left/counterculture was also disenchanted with and concerned about the loss of individualism. The Beat movement of the 1950s, in the tradition of Emerson, Thoreau, and Whitman, cast a modern representation of "expressive individualism." This concept holds that each person has a unique essence of feeling and intuition that should be allowed to unfold or be expressed if individuality is to be realized (Bellah et al. 1985, 33–35). The Beats, through their lifestyle featuring sex, drugs, jazz, and material simplicity, repudiated middle-class culture's incessant drive for wealth in favor of a deeper cultivation of the self. In the early 1960s, several signs of this expanding expressive individualism could be detected, from comedian Lenny Bruce to liberalized pornography laws, pop art, and New York's Living Theatre.

Kimble's situation as a middle-class American falsely accused, convicted, and sentenced to death by a system he still supports, expresses the deep-seated anxieties of the era—the fear that society's institutional systems will erode and eventually eradicate individual autonomy. Kimble is caught in a double-bind. On the one hand, his fugitive status liberates him and enables him to escape from the stifling conformity of his former suburban life. On the other hand, he is unable to fully assert his individualism for fear that his true identity will be discovered by the authorities. Kimble must conform to and blend into the background of everyday life. He is a man resigned to living outside established society in order to retain his freedom. He is a Kafkaesque victim of an overrationalized, bureaucratic justice system that refuses to acknowledge his innocence and seeks to destroy him. Because Kimble refuses to submit to the will of the system, his stance represents an affirmation of individualism.

The Fugitive's narrative structure closely follows the familiar patterns of mythic individualism. Like the American cowboy, Kimble is an outsider, existing on the margins of traditional society, who enters a community each week and helps its inhabitants rid themselves of evil forces so that they can grasp their own moral worth. But, unlike the cowboy, Kimble's outsider status is not his choice but society's. In the course of assisting alienated individuals, he helps them assert their own individuality against the suffocating conformity of society.

Over the past hundred years, individualism has been closely related to middle-class status. Because the primary focus of this group is status mobility, many of the most productive features of U.S. society appear to be "the normal outcome of individual achievement" (Bellah et al. 1985, 148–49). As an educated, upwardly mobile professional, Kimble is a product of this type of middle-class individualism. This differs from expressive individualism in that its primary emphases are social status, upward mobility, and wealth accumulation rather than personal expression. As a fugitive, Kimble retains some of its tenets but also exhibits the nonmaterialistic aspects of expressive individualism.

There is, however, an essential contradiction at the heart of American individualism. There is a deeply held fear that society may overwhelm the individual and destroy his or her chance for autonomy. However, it is only in relation to society that the individual can achieve complete fulfillment. Kimble's plight expresses this inner conflict. His constant travel provides him with a small measure of human companionship, although he can never really become a part of any community without risking revealing his identity. He must stay on the run to maintain his freedom. After all, it was his own community that wrongfully convicted him as a murderer.

In the episode "Devil's Carnival," Tad (Dee Pollack), a teenage boy, befriends Kimble after he saves him from being hit by a truck driven by Hanes McClure (Warren Oates), the town's near legendary criminal. Tad subsequently helps Kimble escape from the local jail. The boy, suffocating from his mother's attention and the conformity of the small town, displays his youthful wanderlust by giving Kimble a copy of Whitman's *Leaves of Grass*. The scene is one of the earliest references to expressive individualism in the series. As is evident from the episode's title, the community here is represented as a grotesque, hellish vision of crass commercialism and wanton sin. Shirky Saulter (Strother Martin), who owns the town's pool hall, capitalizes on both Kimble's and McClure's notoriety by selling peeks of their jail cells and has a beautiful blonde pose next to the hall's bullet holes while jacking up the price of beer and coffee.

At the end of the episode, Kimble tells Tad that if he must leave, he should "walk like a man, not run" (Bellah et al. 1985, 150–51). In the final scene Tad leaves both his mother and the town behind him. Although everyone faces separation and individuation, the concept of leaving home is a particularly American one. In a few Western European countries, the issue is not leaving home but rather remaining home to take care of one's parents until their death as well as honoring one's ancestors. In the United States young adults are expected to leave home in order to attain personal autonomy and a sense of self. In the context of this episode, in order for the boy to grow up he must leave not only his family but also his community. Community is represented as an obstacle to the boy's growth in the episode rather than a means of providing him with a sense of social commitment and continuity. The episode's resolution expresses television's familiar version of realism, which is closely aligned with individualism. Most narrative problems are personalized through individual characters and are resolved through individualized actions (Fiske 1987, 152–53). Thus, in the case of the troubled boy, the problem can be solved by a single action and the solution is found through individuals rather than society. *The Fugitive*'s typical bourgeois narrative focus on the significance of the actions of the individual implicitly negates the role of other factors, such as social class, race, and gender, that underscore many of society's problems.

The community is also characterized as socially confining and repressive while hiding a dark streak of violence in the episode "The Witch" (9/24/63). Emily Norton (Patricia Crowley), an unmarried schoolteacher, is the victim of malicious gossip in a small rural community. After a story circulates about her romantic encounter with Kimble, the town elders vote to run her out of town. At the last minute, Kimble steps forward with the truth that there was no romantic affair, only to have the town unleash its violent rage against him. In the end, Norton and the town folk forge an uneasy alliance. Although she agrees to stay for the sake of the children, the community is a continuing threat to her personal freedom. Norton's contradictory situation reflects the inherent ambivalence within the values of individualism and community. The episode's story of a socially repressive small community punishing a nonconformist person shares affinities with Arthur Miller's play *The Crucible* (1953), based on the 1692 Salem witch trials. Both the play and the episode serve as cautionary tales about the perils of gossip and the vengeful nature of the community on the nonconformist.

Kimble frequently travels to small towns that exist on the very margins of society. These images of small-town America serve as effective narrative economy and reflect Kimble's nostalgic memories of his own hometown. Emanuel Levy argues that small towns in 1950s films began to receive a more critical portrayal, as ordinary life in them was represented "as emotional stifling, intellectually suffocating, and sexually repressive," as evident in such films as *All That Heaven Allows* (1955), *Peyton*

Place (1957), and *Picnic* (1955) (1991, 143–46). Because social conformity is a recurring theme in Hollywood family melodramas, the stories tended to be situated in small towns (Schatz 1991, 151). Despite these critical representations, which continued unabated in the early 1960s, film and television narratives still propagate a patriarchal ideology, which organizes sexual difference within their patriarchal order (Levy 1991, 117–29). Despite *The Fugitive*'s often harsh portrayals of small-town America, cities are seen as generally devoid of even the possibility of community.

The Fugitive also suggests that even radical individualism has its limitations. In the episode "The Shattered Silence" (4/11/67), Kimble encounters two self-styled individualists, Andrea Cross (Antoinette Bower), a free-spirited sculptor, and John Mallory (Laurence Naismith), a hermit. At the beginning of the episode, Cross offers Kimble a job and invites him to stay at her home. Kimble asks her why she would invite a strange man into her home, and she responds by saying that "life is short, you have to trust yourself and what you feel about people." Later that same night, Cross invites Kimble into her bedroom. Cross's instinctual, open manner coupled with her bohemian lifestyle make her character a symbol of other expressive individualists, such as the Beats and the hippies.

The other character Kimble meets has taken individualism to its most radical form. Kimble, wounded by a police gunshot, is rescued by Mallory. The hermit has lived away from civilization for the previous fourteen years and claims that he does not need the "real" world; he has created his own private world in the woods. Referencing Thoreau as a man who chose to live outside society, Mallory denies suffering from any loneliness, contending that his dogs and the woods keep him company. But as Kimble's wounds heal, the hermit increasingly becomes reluctant to let him leave the cabin. When Mallory becomes seriously ill, Kimble redeems the old man's faith in humanity by risking his own capture to bring back medicine from a pharmacy. Although Mallory and Cross do not know each other, at the episode's end, these two strong-willed individualists find they have much in common as Cross decides to stay with the old man to nurse him back to health. The episode suggests that radical individualism taken too far will ultimately lead to loneliness and despair. When individualism is not connected to community, it becomes a form of asocial or antisocial behavior. *The Fugitive* leaves little doubt that when Kimble finally finds the one-armed man and is cleared of the murder charges, he will willingly return to his place within his community.

Love and Marriage

Concerns about the pressures of social conformity extend to the realm of marriage. Kimble's troubled marriage is central to the premise of the series and seemed to serve as an implicit cause for his unjustified conviction and exile. On the very night of Helen Kimble's death, Richard fought with her over whether they should adopt a child. Helen, who lost the ability to have a child because of a miscarriage, argued that adopting a child would be "living a lie." Helen's concern expresses the intense pressures many women felt to become traditional mothers. Richard's interest in adoption is both personally and socially conformist. Many *Fugitive* episodes illustrate these heightened social tensions and their effects on marriage, family, and relationships.

During the 1960s, just about every institution—including marriage—was scrutinized for its role in either facilitating or impeding the search for personal freedom. Several cultural developments—a more sexually permissive society, expanded social mobility, and the renewed quest for personal liberty—placed even greater strains on the institution of marriage. Although marriage remained the norm, the divorce rate began to climb. Without the support of religious beliefs and economic necessity, marriage and family would not survive as "normally" constituted, especially in an era that placed such a high value on individualism. Richard Rapson argues that within an increasingly individualistic society, marriages had come, for many, to represent a type of prison in which people are unable to experience personal growth and freedom (1988, 126–27).

Americans have traditionally viewed adulthood with fear that is connected to an underlying ambivalence about romantic love. The power of the love myth is in its perceived ability to bind together contrasting elements (e.g., individual rebellion, sexual expression, self-restraint) into a single unified social entity—marriage—that promised to resolve any conflicts among these behaviors. These conflicts, however, are a symptom of the tension existing in the United States between the freedom of the individual and the social demands of society. Although the myth of romantic love has upheld the ideals of enduring love and commitment, these ideals have been under attack from America's culture of aggressive individualism (Swidler 1980).

In the early 1960s, writers began to bring this ambivalence out into the open. Betty Friedan's best-seller *The Feminine Mystique* (originally published in 1963) expressed the growing dissatisfaction that many women felt in their socially prescribed role as housewife. She defined "the feminine mystique" as the notion that a woman can be fulfilled only as a wife and a mother. Friedan describes the signs of women's discontent in the rise of divorces, neurosis, and unhappiness. She says that by 1962, "the plight of the trapped American housewife had become a national parlor game" (2001, 70).

Barbara Ehrenreich argues that since the 1950s, men have resisted the "breadwinner ethic" that made them the dominant economic providers for the family. She asserts that various social movements (largely generated by men) have emerged since the 1950s, each defining a flight from the male provider image. In the 1950s, for example, there were attacks on social conformity and "*The Man in the Gray Flannel Suit* (1955) mentality," such as the celebratory and consumerist bachelor male model and the beatniks, who rejected both work and marriage (1983, 14–67, 99–116). *The Fugitive* also presented a flight from the male provider image. Although Kimble is in a state of constant paranoia and fear, his fugitive status frees him from the middle-class commitments of work, marriage, and family. As a fugitive, he can never sustain a long-term relationship, hold a steady job, or fully assimilate into a community.

The debate over the status of marriage as an institution was the topic of several *Fugitive* episodes. In "The Girl from Little Egypt," for example, Kimble's former marital life is contrasted with a young woman's affair with a married man. One night, Ruth Norton (Pamela Tiffin), a flight attendant, distraught over discovering that her gentleman friend is married, hits Kimble with her car. Kimble is rushed to a nearby hospital. At the hospital, Kimble's unconscious state allows for a flashback to the fateful events leading up to his wife's murder, his trial and conviction, and his escape from the derailed train en route to his execution. The flashbacks reveal that his wife had had a stillbirth and lost the ability to bear children. Later, one evening, the Kimbles fight about adoption.[4] Frustrated, Richard leaves home only to return to find Helen's (Diane Brewster) dead body on the floor. The episode's flashback sequence is perhaps the most stylistically expressive in the series. We see from Richard's viewpoint on an ambulance gurney as it slowly dissolves into a scene of him, with prematurely gray hair, talking to Helen's doctor. The scene is also aurally complex; as it dissolves we hear a male voice repeating the phrase "We did everything we could" several times. When the scene finally comes into focus for the viewer, we learn that it is Helen's doctor who has said the phrase, as part of his explanation of their efforts to save the life of Kimble's newborn. The visual pattern of beginning with Kimble's point of view and proceeding into a fluctuating, slow dissolve into past events is repeated throughout his hospital stay to reveal to the audience key events that led to his fugitive status. These distinctive scenes also provide the audience with

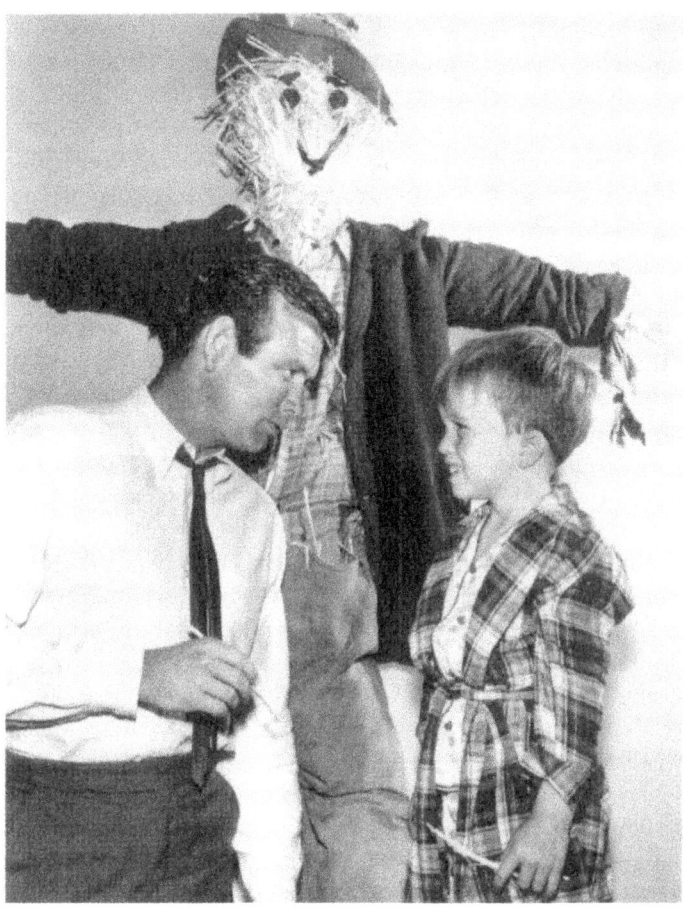

Kimble (Janssen) as Chris Benson befriends Johnny (Clint Howard) in the 1965 episode "Set Fire to a Straw Man."

a brief glimpse into Kimble's tortured unconscious, which is haunted by the events that led up to his wife's murder.

After a few days, the doctor agrees to release Kimble to convalesce at Norton's home. Once he recovers, the fugitive chastises the flight attendant and opens her eyes to the futility of continuing an affair with a married man. Finally, Kimble leaves her with the hope that in time she'll be rewarded with both a loving husband and children. Despite its bittersweet resolution, the episode contains several complex observations about relationships and modern marriage, each delivered with a touch of hard-boiled cynicism. Kimble, portrayed as a man of worldly wisdom, describes Norton's affair as a familiar scenario, "the old story of the lonely girl in the big city." Kimble and Norton recite, almost in unison, a predictable tale of the married man who calculatingly takes her to a restaurant aptly known as "one of those little hide-a-ways that traps ten women a week." Kimble depicts her married boyfriend as a particular type of man and "the city's full of them—they're a lot like children. . . . I want, I want—all pleasure, not pain. If someone gets hurt, it won't be them. They'll always find someone else."

Kimble's description of deceitful married men as predatory beasts represents a growing societal concern over the instability of marriage as a social institution. At a time of declining birthrates, a dramatic surge in divorce rates, and a proliferation of single-parent households, many Americans feared that these were symptoms of increasing selfishness and self-centeredness, which were incompatible with strong family values (Mintz and Kellogg 1988, 204–5). Kimble's reference to these married men as "children" illustrates Ehrenreich's argument that certain social sanctions are used against men, even by other men, to encourage them to accept their responsibilities as husbands and fathers, and to adhere to the ideal of the male breadwinner. These sanctions include accusations of immaturity, effeminacy, and homosexuality, which serve to stigmatize men and castigate them for being irresponsible (Ehrenreich 1983, 14–28). The presence of these deceptive married men shows that bourgeois marriage cannot contain the libidinous desires of men or women.

At the same time, the effeminacy mentioned above implicitly reinforces the notion that women are feminine and helpless, and thereby permanently immature. The episode's depiction of young women as vulnerable, unwitting victims of prowling married men reinforces the patriarchal view of women as socially dependent. *The Fugitive*'s women are represented as both temporary romantic interests for Kimble and dependent victims in dire need of male protection and wisdom. In Kimble's case, his own marital conduct is at the core of his dilemma. At his trial, his neighbors testified that they heard several heated disputes between Kimble and his wife, and later saw her with physical signs of a struggle. Through circumstantial evidence and Kimble's own lack of remorse, the jury simply filled in the gaps and found him capable of committing murder. Other views of the lives of married couples in the suffocating suburbs may be found in contemporary popular novels such as John Cheever's *The Housebreaker of Shady Hill* (1958) and John Updike's *Rabbit, Run* (1960).

The road to a stable marriage or relationship is a perilous, rocky one in the episode "Detour on a Road Going Nowhere." A detour leaves a group of lodge guests stranded along a roadside when their bus breaks down. Following a news report that reveals his identity, Kimble is tied up and held prisoner until the police arrive. Two women and their dilemmas are contrasted in the narrative: Louanne Crowell (Elizabeth Allen), a young, jaded woman in search of a reason to continue to engage in intimate relationships, and Enid Langer (Phyllis Thaxter), a middle-aged wife struggling to hold her shaky marriage together. Crowell has been so severely hurt in past romances that she has developed a cynical, hardened attitude toward men and marriage. Distressed by her inability to establish a relationship with Kimble, she flirts with an older man. In the end, despite her knowledge of Kimble's identity, his quiet strength and courage persuade her to renounce her scorn for men and she decides to help him escape. The episode reinforces the patriarchal notion that for a woman to achieve happiness, it is chiefly a matter of the "right man" coming along and changing her life.

Enid fights to maintain her longstanding marriage with her philandering husband, Ted (Lee Bowman). At the beginning of the episode, Ted is seen flirting with Crowell in full view of his wife. Confronting him, Enid tells him, "You've reached middle age, that's not a disease, it's a fact of nature. I can't stay here and watch you still trying to prove you're a rollicking youth." Ted accuses her of delivering too many meaningless ultimatums and offers to send her home once the bus returns to the lodge. Ted is in the midst of a midlife crisis, in which adults reevaluate their values and goals, contend with their own deaths, and plan the second half of their lives (Jacques 1965). Ted's character reinforces the stereotype of the middle-aged man who must prove his virility by chasing younger women. By the end of the episode, Enid has learned from watching Crowell's self-sacrificing assistance to Kimble to fight to keep her husband. To help Kimble, Crowell pretends to seduce Ted in order to allow Kimble time to escape. Later, confronting Crowell, Enid has renewed her resolution to save her troubled marriage. One of the options for the couple not considered in the story is divorce. In fact, throughout the series, divorce is never featured as a resolution to an unhappy marriage. Quinn Martin says that, at the time, he did not believe in representing divorce as an acceptable alternative to marital problems. In the early 1960s, divorce was still a subject rarely addressed in prime-time television.

Philip Gerard's wife, Marie (Barbara Rush), is a disenchanted, marital fugitive in the two-part episode "Landscape with Running Figures" (11/16/65, 11/23/65). As the episode begins, Gerard has diverted his and Marie's vacation to participate in yet another police dragnet designed to capture Kimble. After being left alone waiting in her hotel room, Marie decides to assume a new identity and take a bus back to her hometown. During the bus trip, a sudden accident leaves her temporarily blind, and Kimble, a fellow bus passenger, rushes her to the nearest town to find medical assistance. Eventually, when Marie discovers that he is Kimble, she tries everything to hold him until her husband arrives. Within the episode, Marie projects all of her deeply felt rage concerning her own life and marriage onto Kimble. She blames Kimble for her troubled marriage, though it's apparent that his presence only masks a deeper range of marital problems. Throughout the episode, for example, Marie and Philip appear unable to communicate their feelings to each other. At the beginning of the episode, Marie is painfully hurt over her husband's decision to divert their vacation, whereas he remains insensitive to her emotional needs and is only concerned with Kimble. At the end of the episode, as she recovers in a hospital room, Gerard, still distracted by the fact that he has lost track of Kimble yet again, is uninterested in her experiences. He comforts her by saying, "We can all go back as if nothing had happened." Marie, speaking in a monotone, repeats his statement, "Nothing happened." In an ironic final shot of the couple, the camera zooms in on them clasping their hands together with wedding bands exposed as if to note that she is grudgingly resigned to stay in their marriage.

This episode highlights the effects of careerism, which was bred by the postwar bureaucratization of work and the demands of corporate life. Men who find their family lives unsatisfying or problematic, or who are anxious about the family budget often compensate by losing themselves in their jobs, subordinating everything in pursuit of their careers. Gerard is so obsessed with capturing Kimble that when his stranded wife finally gets an open phone line to talk to him, he is completely enraged by her interference with his manhunt. Even though he later apologizes to her, it is clear that his career takes precedence over his marriage and family responsibilities.

Culture of Professionalism

Societal concerns about marriage and careerism were closely allied to anxieties over the growth of the culture of professionalism and its influence over personal choice and freedom. John F. Kennedy's election brought America its first buttoned-down, management-style president. The culture of professionalism seemed to be at its pinnacle with the decade's achievements in space exploration and other technological feats. At the same time, many observers were concerned about the public's increased reliance on experts and professionals in almost every walk of life. They were also disturbed by the notion that creative work from laypersons or nonprofessionals was being supplanted by the onslaught of professionalism. Mary Anne Guitar declares that U.S. society has "made a cult of craft and allowed the pros to infiltrate every corner of life, even its most private areas where the spontaneity of the amateur would surely be more valuable and more appropriate" (1963, 152). She also claims that in every stage of life people are urged to absorb a professional attitude with the implication that if an activity cannot be professionalized one has no right to participate in it or even have an opinion about it.

New Frontier and civil rights reformers also distrusted the tenets of middle-class professionalism. These social reformers sought to lay claim to a set of core values including individual freedom, justice, and social responsibility, which arguably had been overwhelmed by the postwar rush to affluence and technological progress (Sullivan 1995, 116–19). Kimble's victimized, outsider status implicitly associates him with scores of reformers bent on challenging the dominance of established institutions and their drive for greater profits and efficiencies. Also, Kimble's proximity to America's working class places him close to the core American values that many reformers thought were overlooked by institutions employing a bureaucratic approach. Through its narratives, *The Fugitive* supports a humanistic perspective to professionalism in U.S. society. The series asserts that though ethical codes and institutional procedures are essential for effective professional practice, they should never replace individual responsibility or self-identity. *The Fugitive* maintains that professional practice should be aligned with humanistic goals that stress such values as tolerance, compassion, and individual freedom.

Burton Bledstein asserts that the culture of professionalism has become so integrated into "middle-class habits of thought and action" that practically all intelligent individuals conduct their public and private behavior based on it. "Middle class" and "professional" are almost synonymous in American society. Professionalism is more than simply another social institution—it is an external process by which Americans make their lives more rational. It has become a culture, "a set of learned values and habitual responses by which middle-class individuals" shape and articulate their emotional and intellectual needs. Bledstein claims that whenever people have to make crucial decisions about their lives, the culture of professionalism usually wins. Through the culture of professionalism, ambitious Americans structured a society based on "a distinct vision—the vertical vision of career" (Bledstein 1976, ix–x).

Both Gerard and Kimble are examples of middle-class professionals. Gerard typifies a number of the negative aspects linked to professionalism. He is the consummate bureaucratic authority figure. He is completely inflexible; he follows the rigid dictates of the law. His identity is integrated into his position as a law officer. Gerard exemplifies William Whyte's "organization man" in that he has not only given his body and soul to the organization but become "the mind and soul of our great self-perpetuating institutions" (1956, 3). The great peril of this conformity is the way it constrains individuals from acting against the interests of the organization. After Kimble's escape from the train, Gerard steadfastly blames himself for the escape and obsessively pursues him. Gerard's own identity is so wrapped up in his dogged pursuit of Kimble that it takes precedence over his responsibilities to his own family. In two episodes, Gerard cancels a long-promised fishing trip with his son to go on yet another cross-country chase after Kimble. Gerard shows that one of the first casualties of obsessive professionalism is the family.

In his travels, Kimble repeatedly enters into situations where he has to risk revealing his identity in order to help someone needing medical attention. For instance, in the episode "Ill Wind" (3/8/66), Kimble, surrounded by ranch hands who refuse to help, performs a makeshift blood transfusion to save Gerard's life. When questioned by a young woman as to why he would save the life of the man who would send him to his death, Kimble replies that he took the Hippocratic Oath to lend medical care to whoever requires it. The woman and the other ranch hands do not understand Kimble's strict allegiance to a professional code of ethics, a trait he shares with Gerard. In a contradictory expression of professionalism, although Kimble expects Gerard to acknowledge his humane actions, Kimble allows himself only strict obedience to his own ethical standards.

Several episodes of *The Fugitive* tell stories of people caught in crises between their personal values and the ethical standards dictated by their professions. For instance, in the episode "Passage to Helena" (3/7/67), Henry Dalton (Percy Rodriguez), a chief deputy, is a man vainly confident in his inherently superior abilities as a police officer. After Kimble is falsely arrested, Dalton instinctively decides to take him to nearby Helena, Montana, for identification along with a dangerous murderer, Carter (James Farentino), who is scheduled to be executed. Along the way, Dalton is wounded and a fellow deputy is killed in an unsuccessful ambush initiated by two of Carter's friends. Dalton, badly wounded from a gunshot to his leg, marches both Kimble and Carter on the forty-mile trek to Helena. Dalton is grateful to Kimble for the medical attention he receives and offers him an apology in advance if he's proven wrong in holding him but

Lt. Philip Gerard (Barry Morse) and Kimble (Janssen) handcuffed together in the 1966 episode "Ill Wind."

boasts that he's never had to apologize to anyone since he put on a badge. Like Gerard, Dalton's self-identity is tied primarily to his career as a law officer.

After Carter grabs the deputy's gun, Kimble wrestles it away from him and thereby saves Dalton's life. Pointing his shotgun at Kimble, Dalton explains that he cannot let him go but will do everything in his power to make sure he receives a fair trial. Dalton expresses the bureaucratic directive of treating everyone in an impartial manner. Unconvinced, Kimble reminds him that he has a moral choice between his professional obligations and his moral debt to him. Kimble tells him that "A man can do anything he wants to do."

> Dalton: I'm a lawman. If I let you go, I'm nothing.
> Kimble: All right, if shooting me makes you somebody, that's what you've got to do . . . gonna have to shoot me! (*Kimble turns his back and walks away.*)
> Dalton: Kimble! (*He cocks his gun but does not fire.*)

Later, Dalton, humiliated at breaking one of his professional codes in letting Kimble escape, turns in his badge to the sheriff. The sheriff refuses to accept his resignation and tells him, "You're more than a good cop—you're the best man I know and good men are hard to find." The sheriff's statement supports the idea that even a staunch professional should never let his career define his identity.

Although a professional should adhere to a strict code of ethics, *The Fugitive* argues that there are times when some decisions should be based on following one's conscience. At a time in which bureaucratization and professionalism had reached almost every facet of society, this humanistic perspective of separating professional ethics from personal conscience reinforced the ideals of individualism in U.S. society. If it is essential for professionals to maintain a humanistic perspective, it is equally critical that individuals should follow some defined ethical standards within their professions. In the episode "Wife Killer" (1/11/66), Barbara Webb (Janice Rule), a newswire reporter, illustrates the dangers of not abiding by any ethical standards. Webb has led an ambitious but reckless career and we learn

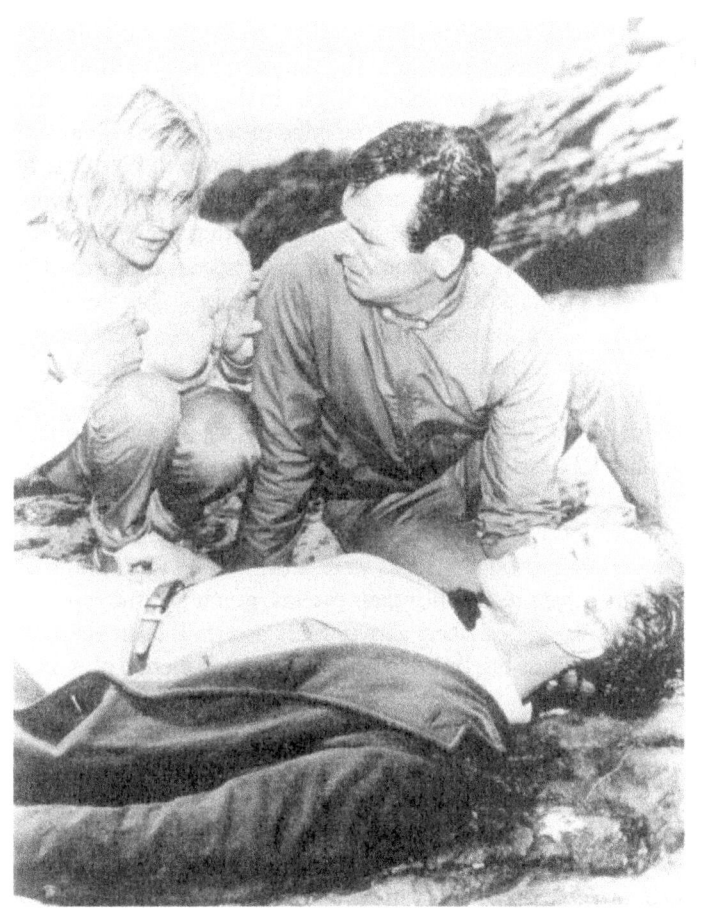

Karen Christian (Susan Oliver) and Jeff Cooper (Kimble) rescue Lt. Gerard (Morse) in the 1963 episode "Never Wave Goodbye, Part 2."

that her fierce desire for the hot story once led to the death of a helpless kidnap victim.

After her photograph of the one-armed man is published, both Kimble and Gerard venture to the police station where he is being held. Upon spotting Kimble, Fred Johnson is frightened and escapes the station. The reporter, noticing Kimble in pursuit, offers to follow Johnson's car. In the ensuing car chase, Johnson's car plummets over the edge of a cliff. With Johnson gravely injured, Kimble is determined to save his life, partly for humanitarian reasons but also because Johnson is the only person who can clear his name. The reporter, however, demonstrating her lack of humanity and professional ethics, is only concerned with obtaining the exclusive rights to Kimble's story in exchange for assistance in saving Johnson's life. Her unethical behavior includes taking advantage of her friendship with her former editor in order to lose the police who have been following her. Webb's most fraudulent act occurs when, believing that Johnson has died, she forges his signature on a signed confession saying that he murdered Kimble's wife.

During the postwar era, many social critics began to notice that certain personality types were more willing to lie and manipulate others to advance their careers, much like the reporter in the episode described above. Mills asserts that in the corporate world of big business, the private conscience of white-collar workers is weakened and a "higher immorality" is institutionalized. When business transactions become impersonal, business executives begin to feel less responsible for their actions. Mills argues that older codes and values no longer hold sway with the men and women of our present corporate era, nor are there any new codes and values that give meaning to their work and life (1970, 343–61). Because ordinary citizens have no firm social or cultural frames by which to identify and understand their own place in history and society, the monetary values of the marketplace command their lives.

Unlike the reporter, Kimble expresses both strong professional and personal concern over preserving Johnson's life. When he discovers that Webb has forged Johnson's signature, he is even more anxious about the prospect that Johnson might die. At the episode's end, the reporter, after witnessing Kimble's decency toward the man who killed his wife, seems to have discovered some ethics. Back at the police station, Webb admits to aiding Kimble and attempts to convince Gerard of his innocence. Johnson, however, the only witness to her crime, escapes from the city hospital and leaves town. *The Fugitive* asserts that though professionals should adhere to a clear code of ethics, there are circumstances in which one needs to follow one's conscience. People should never be completely defined by their professions and institutional values.

Modern Science and Technology

The Fugitive argues that scientific research and technological innovation should always be tempered by an ethical perspective that takes into account the well-being of people. The 1960s witnessed the increasing impact of modern science and technology on American lives. These scientific and technological developments include Theodore Maiman's perfection of laser technology for medical and industrial purposes, NASA's launch of the first communication satellite Echo 1A, and its successful manned space programs. Writers such as C. E. Ayres believed that Americans in the early 1960s were living in the golden age of scientific enlightenment and artistic achievement. Ayres insisted that science and technology would bring about progress and that the industrial society it helped create was the only kind of society in which the great values of western man—freedom, equality, security, excellence, and abundance—can be fully realized (1965).

Jacques Ellul, on the other hand, was deeply disturbed by modern science's obsession with "technique" that, as he defines it, encompasses not only technological methods but the subservience of humans to technology. Technique establishes the domination of standardization over human nature and of means over ends, thereby leading to the corruption of moral values and the eventual dehumanization of society. Ellul claims that in order for science to reach its utopian goals (e.g., space travel, freedom from disease and famine, inexhaustible energy resources), the type of society required would be ruled either by a totalitarian group or a dictatorship (1964, 432–36). Critics of science also examined the types of decisions and moral responsibilities faced by scientists and engineers. Theodore Hesburgh, a member of the National Science Board, called for scientists and engineers to become philosophers and question the moral impact of their work. To ask anything less of them would be to reduce scientists and engineers to automatons (1963).

During the 1960s, many observers voiced a growing concern that some scientists were losing a humanistic perspective in their research. U.S. senator William Fulbright believed that scientific goals should be balanced with other social concerns. Although Fulbright acknowledged the significance of space exploration, he argued that it should be joined with other socially pressing goals such as the elimination of poverty and hunger on a global scale (1965, 33–34).

Several episodes of *The Fugitive* explore the moral and social responsibilities of Kimble's former medical colleagues and other scientists. The episode "Death Is a Very Small Killer" (3/21/67) reveals the unethical behavior of a scientist bent on finding the cure for a deadly strain of meningitis plaguing a small Mexican town. Dr. Howell's (Arthur Hill) obsession is so overwhelming that Reina Morales (Carol Lawrence), his fellow doctor and surrogate daughter, accuses him of neglecting his primary duty to the patients at their clinic. Upon Kimble's arrival, Howell, after recognizing Kimble's true identity, blackmails him into assisting with his research and in his daily clinical duties so that he can concentrate exclusively on his medical research. When the doctor discovers that a combination of drugs has produced a cure in his laboratory animals, he wants to test the drugs on the meningitis patients at the clinic. Kimble, however, warns him that the drugs are still listed as experimental and could prove fatal at higher doses. Howell ignores Kimble's warnings and tests the drugs on his patients. Later, Kimble finds out that in order to complete his research, the doctor deliberately withheld lifesaving medication to half of the other meningitis patients. At the end of the episode, Howell lies dying in bed; he has contracted the meningitis strain but is unable to receive his own cure because he has an existing heart condition. The episode presents a portrait of a scientist so blinded by his desire to reach a worthy goal that he cannot see that the methods he employs to achieve it are unethical.

Science is represented as noble and progressive in *The Fugitive*. The scientists, however, are represented as flawed, obsessive people who often lack a clear moral vision. For instance, the episode "Not with a Whimper" (1/4/66) presents the idea that when a scientist does display a social conscience, he or she is apt to be inclined to engage in destructive acts. Dr. McCalister (Lawrence Naismith), Kimble's former hospital mentor, who suffers from a critical heart condition, has become an enraged crusader against air pollution. To gain publicity for his failing campaign, he sets a bomb to explode on the grounds of Hampstead Mills, the town's leading polluter. For melodramatic effect, a group of schoolchildren are touring the factory on the same day the bomb is set to explode. Fortunately, Kimble is able to defuse the bomb before it detonates. The episode depicts the tension between scientists' desire to exhibit a social conscience in their work and the fear that they are ill-equipped to handle the social implications of that work. In *The Fugitive* when scientists do reflect a social conscience in their research, they are often characterized as irresponsible or fanatical. The series confirms the social stereotype that scientists become so obsessed with their research that they are unable to handle the larger social responsibilities associated with their work. This representation expresses the public's dual mistrust and admiration of science. Despite the public's praise of scientific achievements such as space exploration, the proliferation of nuclear weapons and the Cuban Missile Crisis serve as consistent reminders of the lurking, potentially destructive force of advanced technology in the hands of nation-states. As a physician, Kimble has learned to balance his humanity with his medical skills and knowledge. Although Kimble was probably always a caring doctor, it seems that his time on the road, meeting people from all walks of life, has added considerable depth to his compassion as a clinical practitioner.

Social Justice and Authority

The search for individual freedom became intimately tied to the idea of social justice in the forms of liberty and equal opportunity in the 1960s (Clecak 1983, 11–12). Like the main characters on many television westerns of the time, in *The Fugitive* Kimble befriends and assists disadvantaged individuals in order to protect their civil liberties. At the same time, and as with most television crime dramas, *The Fugitive* presented situations that focused on procedural injustices rather than on the distribution of goods and services or the equity of the institutional order of society (Bellah et al. 1985, 334). Several episodes highlight the flaws and inconsistencies in the American justice system. Kimble's wrongful conviction itself highlights the contradictions between justice and the legal system.

By the end of the decade, practically every socially disenfranchised group, in one way or another, had challenged the dominant cultural authority, demanding greater inclusion in the U.S. social and economic enterprise. The changes brought about new debates over the role of authority in society. At the same time, the validity of many U.S. institutions came under closer scrutiny. Issues of inequality and injustice in the United States were becoming more prominent in both the courts and mass culture (Polenburg 1980, 177–78). Under the Warren Court, the criminal justice system underwent a period of liberalization in protecting and ensuring the civil rights of the accused. This liberalization was exemplified in the Supreme

Court's ruling in *Gideon v. Wainwright* (1963) and *Miranda v. Arizona* (1966), which respectively guaranteed the right to legal counsel provided by the state and the right to remain silent in court and in police interrogation.

Elayne Rapping asserts that in the 1960s, a significant number of legal television series featured defense attorneys who often sought to serve the indigent in the interest of social justice and correcting broader social injustices. The best known of these series is *The Defenders* (1961–65), which featured E. G. Marshall and Robert Reed as a father-son legal defense team (2006, 22–23). The popular series dealt with politically charged topics such as abortion, atheism, pornography, civil rights demonstrations, and Hollywood blacklisting (Alvey 2011). *The Defenders* and *Perry Mason* (1957–66) differed from *The Fugitive* in their conceptions of justice and the law. In *Perry Mason*, the tenacious Mason and his legal defense team work to find evidence or an eyewitness that will prove their client innocent in a court of law. The series uses the courtroom as an "idealized" ritualistic space where the truth emerges only after painstaking detective work by Mason's team (Leitch 2005, 26–28). In *The Defenders*, the legal defense team's pursuit of justice takes place within the complex confines of the nation's system of jurisprudence.

In *The Fugitive*, justice is not an ideal or social issue to be fought over by lawyers; it is exclusively in the hands of its victim, such as Kimble, condemned to death by the criminal justice system. The law, for the most part, is portrayed as both the juried courtroom, which found Kimble guilty, and as a menacing, relentless force (primarily) in the form of Gerard. *The Fugitive* contends that justice is a personal matter best left to the individual, not to attorneys and jury trials.

Kimble's personal injustices and empathetic demeanor make him sensitive to people caught in unjust situations. These people tend to be socially disenfranchised and powerless. For instance, in the episode "Glass Tightrope" (12/3/63) Kimble, working as a store clerk at a department store, witnesses his

Lt. Gerard (Morse) faces backwoods justice in the 1965 episode "Corner of Hell." Gerard is confronted by Cody (Bruce Dern) to the right and Tully (R. G. Armstrong) is in the right foreground.

boss, Martin Rowland (Leslie Nielsen), accidently kill a business associate in the store's parking lot. When Kimble finds out that a vagrant found near the store has been charged with the murder, he anonymously phones Rowland to convince him to confess to his crime. Rowland, who mistakenly believes he is being blackmailed, assigns his store detective to find out the identity of the caller. Kimble risks his life to make sure that an innocent man is not tried and convicted for a crime he did not commit. Kimble's status as a social outsider allows him to associate with people from disenfranchised social groups such as drifters, youth gangs, Latino Americans, Native Americans, and African Americans. He does not support their particular social causes but their basic civil rights.

Kimble's unjust conviction provides narrative fodder for examining the inherent flaws and contradictions in the U.S. justice system. The episode "Corner of Hell" (2/9/65), for example, provides an ironic twist on the theme of justice. Kimble and Gerard both find themselves in the company of a clan of southern backwoods bootleggers. When a young woman, Elvie (Sharon Farrell), is gravely injured by one of the men, Cody (Bruce Dern), Gerard is caught in the incriminating position of being discovered next to her fallen body. As a result, Gerard finds himself on trial by the clan's patriarch, Tully (R. G. Armstrong), for the attempted murder of Elvie. Gerard is entrapped by circumstantial evidence and is subsequently condemned to death. Fortunately, Kimble finds Gerard's nearly empty wallet on Elvie and induces her to inadvertently implicate Cody, which saves Gerard from the hangman's noose. Gerard is allowed to leave with the stipulation that he take Elvie to the nearest county hospital.

Despite their obvious differences, the episode highlights the similarities between the U.S. legal system and the clan's version of backwoods justice. After all, within both systems, a preponderance of circumstantial evidence is used to convict both innocent men. In Kimble's case, the combined absence of an alibi and the testimony of witnesses to previous domestic squabbles constituted the state's case against him. In defense of the legal system, Gerard exclaims, "Our system of justice may not be perfect but it does give every man a fair chance to defend himself." Although the U.S. justice system is predicated on the belief that every suspect is considered innocent until proven guilty in a court of law, it is apparent that, in Kimble's case, the burden of proof rested with the accused. In the mock trial, Gerard vents his outrage at the proceedings, exclaiming, "I know very well what you feel, what you think you're trying to do . . . there's not a beast in the jungle that kills for the sake of killing. Stop trying to dignify it and get it over with." Ironically, Gerard's comments point out that both justice systems practice capital punishment even if it is deemed contrary to the laws of nature. The episode's emphasis on the similarities between the U.S. legal system and its cruder wilderness counterpart only serves to stress that ultimately there is little difference between them. Despite the legal system's lofty ideal that every person should be guaranteed a fair trial before an impartial jury, the fact is that an innocent person can still be convicted and sentenced to death. Although Gerard acknowledges that the system is "not perfect," it is clear that its flaws do occasionally condemn an innocent person to death.

Likewise, the theme of ordinary citizens taking justice into their own hands is common in many *Fugitive* episodes. Although this theme is more closely associated with television westerns, it also appears in police and detective dramas. The primary cause of vigilante justice is a strong mistrust of the justice system. *The Fugitive* suggests that this mistrust is most pronounced in small towns. In the 1960s, several films, such as *The Chase* (1966) and *Easy Rider* (1969),[5] began to show the disintegration and decline of communal life and values in small towns. Individuals in these films insist on and succeed in separating themselves from the town's mores. The town no longer possesses the moral authority it once held over its people (Levy 1991, 179–81). With the breakdown of morality, the townspeople become susceptible to flights of paranoia, revenge, and vigilantism. The push for social justice meant tackling concerns about institutional authority. Authority, of course, is essential to enforcing the laws and legal procedures that guarantee equality and liberty for all citizens. Peter Clecak asserts that while self-conscious flights from authority to autonomy are not unique to the American experience, the general disenchantment with authority ran deeper and was more widespread in the 1960s and 1970s, and was perhaps more pervasive than in any other period in U.S. history. Although most Americans realize that some type of authority is necessary to uphold the social order, authority was a social obstacle in the search for personal freedom and social justice. As the 1960s progressed, people seeking greater liberties sought to push back various forms of authority—to get social institutions and other oppressive systems off their backs and to overturn outmoded ideas. By the end of the decade, authority was on the defensive in nearly every sector of U.S. society, including the family, church, university, government, and corporation (Clecak 1983, 277–81).

Authority also became one of the thorniest issues of the civil rights movement. Under the leadership of Dr. Martin Luther King Jr., the movement practiced civil disobedience. Civil rights workers refused to obey unjust laws. As the movement heated up, countless incidents of civil disobedience occurred on both sides, from mass demonstrations to Alabama governor George Wallace's refusal to enforce federal laws. These incidents caused mixed reactions among most Americans concerning the question of whether it is ever appropriate to deliberately disobey the law. In 1964, an article in the Sunday *New York Times Magazine* by the philosopher Charles Frankel expressed the growing concern over this issue, focusing on the question of whether a person has the right to disobey the law if her or his conscience or religious beliefs dictate that the law is unjust. Frankel explains that because not every law is just and because certain governmental authorities can be hostile, sometimes civil disobedience is the only path a minority group can use to attract the attention of the majority to its cause. Frankel, however, does acknowledge that a person's right to break the law cannot be officially sanctioned nor should society give its citizens the freedom to break the law.

Authority is seen as ambiguous in *The Fugitive*. Kimble himself has an ambivalent relationship to it. As a former physician and citizen, he has a strong respect for authority. But as a fugitive, he knows that if he succumbs to authority, he will be executed. The series' central recurring challenge to authority is the way in which individuals from nearly every socioeconomic sector of U.S. society help Kimble escape from the police. A key belief of American individualism is that Americans should rely on their own judgment in forming opinions and in taking certain actions. In episodes of *The Fugitive*, after characters are helped by—or at least bear witness to—Kimble's uncommon humanity, they inevitably assist him in his escape. These challenges to authority usually come from one or only a few people, but in the episode "Nightmare at North Oak" (11/26/63), after Kimble saves a group of schoolchildren from a near tragic bus accident, an entire group of parents become indebted to him. After Kimble rescues the children and driver from the school bus, it explodes, knocking him unconscious. Sheriff Springer (Frank Overton) and his wife offer to take Kimble into their home to recuperate. As Kimble convalesces, the sheriff's son takes his picture and it ends up in the nationwide news, which brings Gerard to town. Springer reluctantly arrests Kimble and agrees to let Gerard extradite him. The townspeople line up at the jail to say a final good-bye to him. The commotion enables one of the people to help him escape. When Gerard demands to know which one of them assisted Kimble in escaping from his jail cell, the whole group joins together in an act of solidarity: they all claim that they aided Kimble.

Authority figures in the series are often portrayed as self-serving and corrupt. Politicians, like Illinois state representative Ballinger (James Daly) in "Running Scared" (2/22/66), want to capture Kimble to further their own political aspirations, not to achieve justice for the death of Helen Kimble. Small-town sheriffs are frequently represented as corrupt, sadistic, and hostile to outsiders. *The Fugitive* resisted Hollywood's inclination, especially pronounced in the 1970s, to stereotype small-town America as a source of evil. The series showed that social prejudice and corruption were systemic in all of U.S. society—city or country. In the episode "A Clean and Quiet Town" (9/27/66), for example, Kimble lands in Clark City, a corrupt gambling city run by a mob syndicate. Fred Johnson, the one-armed man, working as a payoff or bag man, spots the fugitive and hires two corrupt cops to beat him up. Kimble later catches Johnson and attempts to turn him in to the police, only to find out the police are also working for the crime organization. When the mob boss finds out that Johnson paid off the police to beat up Kimble, he must decide what to do with these two troublemakers— kill them or let them go. The mob boss, whose office is located in a modern high-rise office building, is only concerned with maintaining the smooth flow of income into the organization's coffers. The similarities between U.S. business and organized crime explored in the episode are reminiscent of such noir films as Abraham Polonsky's *Force of Evil* (1948) and Fritz Lang's *The Big Heat* (1953). In *Force of Evil*, attorney Joe Morse (John Garfield) works with a gangster to rig a lottery on the Fourth of July so that "the corporation" can take over the local numbers banks and form a profitable monopoly. Morse defends his actions by stating that they are "normal financiers." As with any corporate takeover, the bank workers find themselves alienated from their work and each other. In *The Big Heat*, Detective Bannion (Glenn Ford) avenges his wife's death by taking on a crime syndicate that controls almost every facet of a corrupt city. Years before Coppola's *Godfather* films, *The Fugitive* illustrated how the image of corporate capitalism thoroughly pervaded U.S. popular culture. Despite its illegal activities, the city's syndicate exemplifies modern corporate capitalism taken to its logical extreme: the state's political system becomes completely subservient and beholden to corrupt corporations.

In the episode "Nicest Fella You'd Ever Want to Meet" (1/19/65), Kimble is arrested by the brutally sadistic Sheriff Jo Bob Sims (Pat Hingle) while traveling through a small town in Arizona. Sheriff Sims regularly rounds up and arrests local vagrants so he can use them for slave labor. When Kimble witnesses Sims murder another prisoner and discovers that the town's equally corrupt mayor and town council covered up the crime by calling it an accident, he finds himself in grave danger. Although Kimble should remain detached in such perilous circumstances, he cannot resist attempting to redress an unjust situation. Levy asserts that order and stability in small towns in films of the 1940s and 1950s were typically and satisfactorily represented by policemen, politicians, and other service professionals (1991, 170–81). In *The Fugitive*, however, many of these same authority figures become symptomatic of increased social disintegration, moral corruption, and the abuse of official power. These representations serve as implicit arguments for the need to protect the rights of the accused—and ordinary citizens—against abuses of official authority. This emerging disenchantment with institutional authority came to be expressed with particular power in the noir-inflected *Fugitive*.

The series' humanistic perspective was indicative of broader social movements, such as those to combat poverty and to preserve the environment, which emerged in the 1960s and 1970s with the aim of redirecting the country's institutional matrix toward human-centered goals. This viewpoint is based on the belief that people have the faculty to be compassionate and understanding toward one another. Liberal humanism maintains that, despite their many foibles, humans have the capacity for dignity and indeed nobility. Humanism, with its focus on universal human values, began to lose much of its credibility by the late 1960s. The decade's social and political movements, with their focus on race, gender, class, and sexuality, began to question the idea of timeless universal truths. In the 1970s, a series of domestic and international crises, including the Arab oil embargo, sky-high inflation rates, increased foreign competition, the Watergate scandal, and the Vietnam War, led many Americans to question just how much control and influence they really had over their daily lives. As such, the television wanderer-redeemer began to gradually shift away from a compassionate loner to a more fantastical figure. The wanderer-redeemer began to appear in a variety of fantastic forms: from an angry green-skinned giant with superhuman strength (*The Incredible Hulk* [1978–82]) to a benevolent supernatural angel (*Highway to Heaven* [1984–89]) to a futuristic time-traveling scientist (*Quantum Leap* [1989–93]). These fantastic wanderer-redeemers spoke to people's sense of autonomy and control. The final chapter examines these later wanderer-redeemer series as well as others, along with their thematic and generic relationship to *The Fugitive*.

Chapter 4
The Legacy of *The Fugitive*

On August 29, 1967, the final episode of *The Fugitive* aired on prime-time television. As the newly acquitted Kimble and Jean Carlise (Diane Baker), a court reporter who helped him, walk away from the courthouse, they suddenly spot a police cruiser pulling up alongside them. For a fleeting moment, Kimble's face and body register a strong flush of fear before Carlise gently reminds him to relax. Kimble responds with a half-hearted smile. William Conrad, the omniscient narrator, solemnly states, "Tuesday, August 29th—the day the running stopped." Despite Conrad's somber declaration, you can't help but wonder whether Kimble will ever completely overcome his fear or innate urge to run at the sight of the authorities.

Kimble, of course, was not the only nonviolent wanderer-redeemer on television in the 1960s. However, because of *The Fugitive*'s strong redemptive theme and lasting popularity, it became the most influential wanderer-redeemer series on American television. *The Fugitive*'s main contribution to television culture is establishing the narrative and thematic characteristics that define the contemporary, nonviolent wanderer-redeemer television tradition. The traits of the wanderer-redeemer include: traveling alone or with a partner; having a troubled past and taking to the road because of a momentous event; searching for meaning; and experiencing a troubling relationship with community and society-at-large.

The wanderer-redeemer also serves a Judeo-Christian mythic redemptive role in his journey. Because of his dark past, he is able to empathize with the people he meets who are estranged from their family and friends. The wanderer-redeemer liberates these lost souls through compassion and selfless acts of kindness. Through his actions, the wanderer-redeemer is granted temporary moral redemption for his unfortunate past. While this redemptive role was largely implied in the early television wanderer-redeemer series, as the tradition progressed over time, it became more explicit (see, e.g., *Highway to Heaven*). The wanderer-redeemer's violent dimension is largely suppressed in series' narratives, but he does not hesitate to use physical force if the occasion demands it. Because Kimble is a nonviolent redeemer, he refuses to travel with a weapon and only resorts to physical violence to defend himself or to protect a woman or child. In the first *Fugitive* episode, for example, Kimble rescues a female piano player from further physical abuse by punching her sadistic husband. The violent side of the wanderer-redeemer became more pronounced in the late 1970s and the 1980s, and his character traits, established by *The Fugitive*, continued to shape and influence all of the wanderer-redeemer programs that followed it.

The popular NBC TV series *Run for Your Life*, which overlapped historically with *The Fugitive*, features an interesting and thought-provoking variation on many of the narrative traits and themes established by *The Fugitive*. Roy Huggins, who was aware of all the innocent-man-on-the-run program imitators that followed *The Fugitive*, was approached by NBC to create a new version of the wanderer-redeemer. *Run for Your Life* follows the adventures of Paul Bryan (Ben Gazzara). Bryan runs because his doctor informed him that he has a rare, life-threatening disease for which there is no known cure and that he has at most two years left to live. In this series, *The Fugitive*'s Gerard "is replaced by the specter of Death itself, as Bryan wanders highways and byways in a desperate attempt to discover the meaning of his own essence on the American road" (Marc and Thompson 1992, 149). His sudden awareness of his impending death leads him to sell his law practice, sell his home and possessions, and begin a life of wandering. He hopes to "squeeze twenty years of living into the one or two years he has left." When Bryan leaves the doctor's office, his doctor and the audience learn that there was a mistake—there is nothing wrong with him (Newcomb 1974, 149). Viewers feel a level of tension in all of Bryan's actions because we know they are based on an incorrect medical diagnosis. Gazzara, a theatrically trained New York City actor, plays Bryan as a dynamic man capable of showing both intense bouts of exuberance and melancholy. Because he believes he has a terminal condition, he has a stronger drive to seek new experiences and find the meaning of life than does Kimble. *Run for Your Life*, which emerged in the mid-1960s, seems to capture and express some of the youthful energies and hunger for experience associated with the growing countercultural movements.

Like Kimble, Bryan is a solitary traveler who becomes involved with the people he meets, often romantically, but can never settle in one place because of his conflicted relationship with community. If he joins a community, his existential journey for meaning will end. When Bryan encounters old acquaintances or new people, he does not want to share the knowledge of his imminent death with them in order to avoid straining their relationships. Like Kimble, Bryan can never have any lasting relationships, make a home, or have a family or career. But, unlike Kimble, Bryan has money and does not have to work menial jobs to sustain himself. In fact, he leads a sort of jet-setter lifestyle traveling from one exotic place to another, and even tours the glamour spots of Europe as well as the rural back roads of the United States (Newcomb 1974, 150). Bryan is also

Ben Gazzara as Paul Bryan in the NBC-TV series *Run for Your Life*.

a redemptive figure. His drive for new experiences is balanced by his willingness to help out the troubled people he meets on his journey. Because of what he believes about his own condition, he is extremely empathetic to people who find themselves alienated from life. Bryan knows better than most people that life is short and should be lived to the fullest.

At the end of the 1960s, another wanderer-redeemer series emerged about a man who journeys across the United States on a motorcycle—*Then Came Bronson*. TV critic Jack Gould (1969) labeled this one-season series, which premiered on September 1969, as a "motorized western" in which "the wandering cowboy who once roamed the countryside bestowing compassion and settling problems has been replaced by a helmeted motorcyclist, who both worships his machine and assists his fellow man." Bronson's Harley-Davidson Sportster motorcycle serves as an expressive symbol of unbridled freedom from the oppressive responsibilities of a conformist society. With the popularity of outlaw biker films such as *The Wild Angels* (1966) and *Easy Rider* (1969), the motorcycle became an emblem of the 1960s counterculture movement.

Then Came Bronson's story concept is that Jim Bronson (Michael Parks) has dropped out of mainstream society and wanders the countryside in order to discover a more fulfilling life. Bronson takes to the road after his best friend commits suicide under the Golden Gate Bridge in San Francisco. Bronson quits his job as a newspaper reporter, divests himself of his material possessions, and leaves town on his friend's motorcycle. He escapes for a life on the road to ponder the meaning of life and to free himself of the traditional bonds of a middle-class life. The series' opening begins with Bronson leaving San Francisco on his bike and meeting an exhausted commuter in a station wagon waiting at a red light. The commuter asks him where he is going and Bronson says, "I don't know. Wherever I end up, I guess." The beleaguered businessman looks longingly at the bike and declares, "Man, I wish I was you." Bronson shrugs and says, "Really? Well, hang in there." The show's opening expresses the series' thematic premise and Bronson's existential search for a simpler life away from the confinements of the big city and all the social trappings of a bourgeois existence. Similar to Bryan, Bronson's search for the meaning of life is more explicit than Kimble's journey.

Despite his quest for self-discovery, Bronson serves a moral liberator role in the series in that he helps alienated people in psychological crises. Similar to Kimble, Bronson must stop along the road and take an odd job for a few days to support himself. In these breaks, he meets a diverse range of socially powerless and psychically wounded souls existing on the margins of mainstream society. In the series' first episode, "The Runner" (9/17/69), for example, Bronson lends a helping hand to mentally disturbed children, in particular an autistic boy named John (Mark Lester) known as "the runner" because of his inclination to flee. Bronson uses the boy's fascination with his motorcycle to coax him out of his shell. Like Kimble, Bronson is able to tap into his own psychological pain to empathize with and aid characters who are in desperate need of compassion (Gould 1969). Bronson's free-spirited, expressive individualistic character helped alleviate any middle-class anxieties about countercultural hippies by showing the good-hearted benevolence at the core of this character-type. While Bronson has several romantic relationships, close friendships, and offers to join the communities he visits, he refuses, knowing that to settle down would put an end to his spiritual wandering. Parks, a Method actor like Janssen and Gazzara, gives a moody, sensitive performance in his loner role as Bronson. Parks even sung the series' closing theme song, "Long Lonesome Highway," which became a hit song in 1970.

By the mid-1970s, a cultural shift occurred in popular culture whereby the wanderer-redeemer moved from being a marginal outsider to a full-fledged fantasy figure. Andrew Britton (1986) defines this shift toward adult fantasy-style entertainment as "Reaganite entertainment." In this era of reassuring sequels and repetitions, popular films featured benevolent extraterrestrials, such as *E.T.* (1982), and comic-strip-style adventurers, such as *Star Wars* (1977), *Superman* (1978), and *Raiders of the Lost Ark* (1981). These films construct the adult spectator as a child partly to diminish many of the ideological contradictions residing in the storylines and to provide a measure of self-satisfying indulgence (Wood 1986, 162–80). These movies also affected television programming with the advent of such high-concept, fantasy-style series as *The Incredible Hulk, The A-Team, Beauty and the Beast* (1987–90), *Highway to Heaven*, and *Quantum Leap*. Robin Wood argues that this trend was part of a national movement toward psychological reassurance following such traumatic events as the Vietnam War and the Watergate scandals, stressing that an implicit intent of this entertainment was to defuse and render safe all the major radical movements of the 1960s and 1970s: radical feminism, black militancy, and gay liberation (1986, 162–80).

The television series *The Incredible Hulk* is based on the popular comic book series (1962–2008) of the same name published and distributed by Marvel Comics. *The Incredible Hulk*'s central premise, which is somewhat different from that of the comic book, is that one of Dr. David Banner's (Bill Bixby) experiments on the effects of adrenaline on human strength with radiation goes terribly wrong and he ends up creating a raging, green-skinned alter ego played by Lou Ferrigno. Banner's physical transformation and the destruction of his lab serve as the main catalysts for his journey. While the primary objective of his journey is to find a cure for his peculiar affliction, it is also an unstated inner search for meaning and a reason to live, especially with his condition and the untimely death of his wife.

Similar to Gerard's role in *The Fugitive*, Jack McGee, a tabloid reporter, relentlessly pursues Banner. McGee wants to reveal the truth about the appearance of the raging green-skinned creature in order to revive his stagnating career. Kenneth Johnson, the series producer, admits that Jack Colvin's unrelenting portrayal of McGee is modeled on Javert in *Les Misérables* (Rathwell 1998). McGee's recurring presence in the series serves as a constant reminder to Banner of his anguished past; it also serves as another reason for him to stay on the run in search of a cure for his affliction.

In *The Incredible Hulk,* Banner serves a redemptive role in that he helps people resolve their personal crises so they can take responsibility for and determine their own futures. Because of his seemingly incurable condition and the death of his wife, he sympathizes with the distressed and often powerless souls he meets in his travels. However, unlike prior wanderer-redeemers, Banner's character expresses traits of both nonviolent and violent redeemers. Banner, a conscientious, former professional, relies on compassion and reason in most situations. But if the situation cannot be resolved through reason and if his inner aggression is aroused, the Hulk resolves things through brute force. Through the conventions of science fiction, the long-suppressed aggression of the nonviolent wanderer-redeemer is allowed to surface as the Hulk. The appearance of Banner's alter ego seems to argue that reason and compassion have their limits and that some conflicts require violent resolutions. As with other wanderer-redeemers, Banner has a conflicted relationship with the communities he visits. Each community provides him with another chance to discover a possible cure for his affliction, to enjoy a little human companionship, and to contemplate his turbulent past. But because his condition is unpredictable and cannot be completely controlled, he cannot join a community. In *The Incredible Hulk*, the world is constructed as a corrupt, unscrupulous place where most personal crises are resolved only through the actions of a supernatural being.

In the NBC series *Highway to Heaven,* the formerly implicit Judeo-Christian mythic redemptive role of the wanderer-redeemer is made manifest in the series' main character, Jonathan (Michael Landon), a probationary angel and direct agent of God. The series follows Jonathan's divine mission on earth to bring love and understanding into the lives of troubled individuals. While Jonathan has angelic powers, he seldom uses them, preferring to rely on persuasion and example as he inserts himself into people's lives. Similar to *The Fugitive*, *Highway to Heaven*'s episodes tend to focus on the lives of specific individuals and thereby assert that life's problems can only be resolved at the individual not the societal level. Jonathan's probationary status, which is never fully explained in the series, and his direct conversations with "The Boss," as he calls him, move him forward on his journey. Like Kimble, Bronson, and Banner before him, he travels cross-country humbly working as an itinerant laborer. Jonathan's only companion on his journey is a burly ex–police officer named Mark (Victor French), who had been a bitter, defeated man until Jonathan redeemed him with love and compassion and gave him a personal mission (Brooks and Marsh 1988, 343–44).

Because Jonathan is an angel, not a mortal, he cannot fully assimilate into a human community. The relationship between Jonathan as a wanderer-redeemer and society is different from that of previous wanderer-redeemer series like *Route 66* and *The Fugitive*. In *Highway to Heaven*, the world is constructed as cold, spiritually empty, and morally bankrupt. In this setting, personal crises are resolved only through Jonathan's direct divine intervention. Society is represented as increasingly chaotic, while the individual's role in overcoming life's problems has nearly disappeared.

In the 1980s, broadcast network programming became increasingly self-conscious and expressive of its own styles, forms, and history. A progressively sophisticated audience grew more appreciative of stylistic and formal variations along with allusions to its own television history. Throughout *Highway to Heaven*, Landon's Jonathan occasionally pokes good-hearted fun at his angelic role and powers. At the end of one episode, when a retirement home and its patrons are miraculously saved by the winnings from a horse race, Jonathan shrugs his shoulders and remarks, "It's time for me to ride into the sunset" (O'Connor 1984).

NBC's *Quantum Leap* is another program that exemplifies a high degree of self-reflexivity through its blending of the features of both the wanderer-redeemer and science fiction genres. *Quantum Leap* follows the time-travel adventures of Dr. Sam Beckett (Scott Bakula). Because Beckett botched his time-travel experiment, he now spends his days and nights traveling through time—any point between the mid-1950s and the recent past—where he assumes other people's identities. His primary goal is to find a portal that will enable him to return to his own time period, which is slightly into the future. Beckett's journey also serves as an implicit search for meaning and a way to understand his past. In the episode "The Leap Home, Part II" (10/5/90), for example, he travels back to South Vietnam in 1970 for an emotional encounter with his deceased brother, a Navy Seal killed in combat. Beckett's only colleague on his journeys is the wise-cracking, cigar-smoking hologram Al, played with campy fun by Dean Stockwell. Donald P. Bellisario, creator of *Magnum, P.I.* (1980–88) and *N.C.I.S.* (2003–present), created *Quantum Leap,* which seems to have been influenced by a number of time-travel scenarios from the film *Here Comes Mr. Jordan* (1941) to *Highway to Heaven* (Brooks and Marsh 1988, 344).

In *Quantum Leap*, Beckett serves a liberating role in that he meets and helps distressed individuals resolve their dilemmas and thereby change their lives. Similar to Jonathan in *Highway to Heaven*, Beckett has been assigned by an omniscient power, a super hybrid computer known as Ziggy, built by Beckett, to serve as a time-traveling redeemer figure. Al serves as his guide and the interpreter of Ziggy's commands. In previous wanderer-redeemer series the protagonist meets and shares the perspectives of the people he encounters. In *Quantum Leap*, however, science fiction enables the wanderer-redeemer to take his evolving perspective to the next logical extension—he literally becomes different people in his journeys. Beckett takes on such

Admiral Al Calavicci (Dean Stockwell) peers at Dr. Sam Beckett (Scott Bakula) in the NBC-TV series *Quantum Leap*.

disparate roles as an elderly African American man, a young man with Down syndrome, an adolescent hot-rodder, and a female secretary (O'Connor 1989).

Because Beckett, working in conjunction with Al, must

meet a predetermined individual, identify his or her problem, and resolve it within a specific time frame before he experiences a new leap into a new person, he can never really join any of the communities he visits. As with *Highway to Heaven*, Beckett serves a stronger redemptive role as he is able to actually travel back in time to change the course of a person's life. Beckett's redemptive ability to literally change the past is closely associated with the concept of historical revisionism. During the 1980s, President Reagan began redefining various aspects of U.S. society with references to a nostalgic and mythical version of the nation's past: the return to a laissez-faire economy, the reaffirmation of small-town, utilitarian virtues, and the establishment of the Vietnam War as a "just" patriotic war. While *Quantum Leap* is vested with a liberal Hollywood perspective, the series' narrative premise can be associated with this conservative revisionist trend in popular culture, manifested in such Reaganite films as *Back to the Future* (1985) and *Peggy Sue Got Married* (1986), as well as the trend in politics toward revisiting and revising the past along with the perceptions about it.

During the 1990s, the wanderer-redeemer tradition expanded beyond white males to include women, minorities, and a family-like group of protagonists in the CBS series *Touched by an Angel* (1994–2003). John Masius created and Martha Williamson produced the hour-long dramatic series. Masius, who conceived a series with a darker perspective toward humans controlled by a fateful God, was replaced after one season by Williamson, who wanted *Touched by an Angel* to feature more inspirational, life-affirming stories based on Christian values, a perspective that dominated the series to the end of its run (Sterngold 1997). Similar to *Highway to Heaven*, the series' premise is that a trio of angels is sent by God to Earth to help desperate people undergoing a spiritual and psychological crisis realize that God loves them and has not forgotten them. The main characters include Monica (Roma Downey), an apprentice angel, Tess (Della Reese), a veteran angel, Monica's supervisor, Andrew (John Dye), the Angel of Death who appears when people die to take them to heaven or hell, and Gloria (Valerie Bertinelli), an inexperienced angel learning about human suffering and happiness who joined the show for the final two seasons. Tess and Andrew help Monica learn the ropes as an apprentice angel or caseworker. Monica, in the course of her pathway to full-fledged angel, learns firsthand about the desires, struggles, and miseries of humans.

The group of angels became one of television's many primetime "television families." The ascetic solitude of the wanderer-redeemer's journeys was replaced by the warm camaraderie and support of a company of angelic coworkers and supervisors. This group of dedicated, hard-working angels shares commonalities with other ensembles of fictional television professionals and their audiences. As with previous wanderer-redeemers, the angels primarily focus on assisting the socially powerless and marginalized (e.g., women, children, the mentally challenged, the homeless). Kimble and Bronson are often ambivalent about the social demands of family and often assert that a person must leave home to find one's true place in life. In *Touched by an Angel*, however, the stories tend to be centered on preserving or forming a traditional, heterosexual family. In the episode "Manny" (12/14/94), for example, Monica persuades Dr. Harrison (Robin Thomas), a prim doctor who is shaken to the core when he discovers that his family's ancestry is not as prestigious as he once thought, that God loves him and leads him to the hiding place of Luis (Jonathan Hernandez), a young, Hispanic homeless boy. Harrison and his wife decide to adopt the boy and become a family. In the series, family becomes an all-encompassing social and spiritual balm, a place to return to when people find themselves in trouble or adrift in life. *Touched by an Angel* does not admit that families can be a source of long-term conflicts or that despite their rewards and pleasures, family relations can serve as a barrier to individual freedom.

Since the series' main characters are angels, not mortals, they cannot assimilate into the communities they visit in their missions. As with *Quantum Leap*, the angels have a stronger salvation role than do earlier wanderer-redeemers. The angels encounter individuals who live in an impersonal world filled with suffering and hardships where it seems only the act of divine intervention can alter a person's fate. These people cannot rely solely on their families, friends, or even the kindness of a wandering stranger to help them in their moment of personal crisis. *Touched by an Angel*'s stories implicitly suggest that society and its institutions have been simply too powerful and pervasive for individuals to determine their own destinies.

The Fugitive: **The Movie**

In 1993, Warner Brothers Pictures released a film version of *The Fugitive* based on the original television series. The studio decided to produce the film because of the continued popularity of the original series and the corporate production trend of producing films based on existing copyrighted properties, such as TV series, comic books, and video games. The successful *Fugitive* film, directed by Andrew Davis, grossed over $368 million worldwide (Fugitive 2009). In the film, the esteemed Chicago surgeon Dr. Richard Kimble (Harrison Ford) arrives home to find his wife, Helen (Sela Ward), brutally murdered. The police determine that Kimble killed his wife, and he is arrested, tried, convicted, and sentenced to death. However, on the way to prison, Kimble's bus crashes, and he escapes and goes on the run, only to be pursued at every turn by Deputy U.S. Marshal Samuel (instead of Philip) Gerard (Tommy Lee Jones). Ford gives an intense, nuanced performance as Kimble, featuring an emotional range that often trembles between fear and rage. Jones's Gerard is a craggy, good-humored character who is slightly amused by his own boastful, verbal declarations.

Unlike the series' stern detective, who conducts a solitary manhunt, the film's Gerard is a well-respected, affable leader of a crack team of federal agents specially trained in catching interstate fugitives. Gerard's character is more complex and ambivalent than it seems at first. As the chase intensifies, he eventually begins to realize that Kimble might be innocent but does not verbalize these new insights to his team. It is not until the end of the film, when Gerard confronts Kimble again, that we fully learn that he is convinced of his innocence. In the film's final scene, Gerard and Kimble share a brief moment of male camaraderie in the back of a police cruiser, a moment they never had in the TV series. After Gerard takes off Kimble's handcuffs, he gently places a towel over the former fugitive's wrists. Kimble quizzically remarks, "I thought you didn't care." Gerard wryly responds, "I don't." Their exchange serves as a playful repeat of an earlier tense moment between them in a tunnel when Kimble confesses his innocence and Gerard patently says that he doesn't care.

Unlike *Quantum Leap* or *Touched by an Angel*, the film did not feature a Reaganite fantasy wanderer-redeemer; rather, it tapped into another popular narrative trend that gained force in the early 1970s: the conspiratorial thriller. This type of thriller features a narrative in which a protagonist investigates a series of brutal crimes and cover-ups and discovers that they are the actions of a small group of people within a large corporation or a governmental agency. In the wake of the Watergate scandal, the conspiratorial thriller expresses deep-seated cultural anxieties about the fragility of the U.S. working and middle classes along with the threat of institutional and corporate bureaucracies on individual freedom and selfhood. Kimble discovers through his own detective work that his wife was murdered by a one-armed man, an ex-police officer, as part of a conspiracy by a multinational pharmaceutical company to remove him from the drug testing trials so as to ensure the smooth FDA approval of its new drug.

Deputy Samuel Gerard (Tommy Lee Jones) contemplates his team's next move in the 1993 film version of *The Fugitive*.

Bennett Kravitz (1999), relying on the work of Frederic Jameson in *The Geopolitical Aesthetic* (1992), suggests that contemporary conspiracies in popular culture serve a psychological function of providing people with a way of imagining the complex totality of global capitalism. Despite their threatening nature, conspiracies provide people with a rationale for the nature of the world and how it works (23–27). While conspiracy films, like *The Fugitive* and *The International* (2009), provide audiences with accessible dramatic frameworks through which they can comprehend facets of global capitalism, they ultimately fall short in critiquing capitalism as an all-encompassing system. The reason they fail is that the group of business co-conspirators or the nefarious corporation represented in these films are ultimately seen as only aberrations within the capitalist system. Since the 1970s, the prevalence of conspiracy narratives in American films speaks to mainstream feelings of political and social helplessness in the face of expanding world capitalism with its vast networks of power and technologies. In the film Kimble is no longer the helpless victim of fate but a disposable element in a complex plan to increase corporate profits. Through its conspiratorial narrative, the film expresses tacit cultural anxieties of middle-class Americans who find their social and economic lives volatile under the domain of global capitalism.

There are several notable differences between the film and the television series. In the film, Kimble is a vascular surgeon who lives in an upscale Chicago penthouse rather than a pediatrician residing in the suburban community of Stafford, Indiana. Whereas in the series Kimble is chased by either Gerard or local law enforcement, the film has him pursued by a team of federal marshals who specialize in apprehending interstate fugitives. The massive national manhunt, the use of the latest surveillance technologies, and Gerard's team make Kimble a much more vulnerable character than he is in the series. *The Fugitive* film effectively illustrates how the sheer power of modern law enforcement and institutional control have increased over time to weaken the autonomy of the individual citizen.

While the film shares some common features with the television wanderer-redeemer tradition, it does not follow the same narrative and thematic trajectories as the series: Kimble does not really journey beyond his hometown and he does not serve as a redemptive force for the people he meets. Ford's Kimble is a hunted, former professional who travels alone in search of redemption. However, with the exception of a young boy in a hospital whom he saves with his medical knowledge, the main thrust of Kimble's actions is not to redeem others but to legally absolve himself by finding out who framed him for his wife's murder. Kimble's fugitive journey in the film is an existential one. Through his experiences, he discovers both his vulnerability and resourcefulness against the powers of corporate medical capitalism. As with the series, there is an implicit sense of youthful liberation for Kimble in his movement. When he alters his appearance to disguise himself by shaving off his beard and dyeing his hair, he appears younger than his former graying self. Kimble, however, does not really serve a Judeo-Christian redemptive role in redeeming his fellow humans. We could argue that Kimble liberates himself and the medical community through his actions to expose the conspiracy. As in the television series, Ford's Kimble suppresses any violent tendencies and refuses to carry a weapon. Ford, who has a firm reputation as a film action hero, provides Kimble with undeniable physical abilities. In the film, Kimble survives a several-hundred-foot jump over a dam into a raging river and an intense shootout in a Chicago subway. Finally, in both the series and the film, Kimble is socially alienated because of his conviction and fugitive status. In the movie, Kimble's status as a social outsider is relatively short compared to the long-running series.

Both the film and the television series express the cultural, bourgeois paranoia associated with their respective time periods. In the 1960s, Kimble's arrest, trial, and conviction reflected the deep-seated cultural anxieties about the fragility of the U.S. middle class and the threat of corporate and governmental bureaucracies on individual freedom and selfhood. The murder of Kimble's wife by Fred Johnson, a lower-class, petty criminal, expresses the middle-class fears of random violence and urban criminality intruding on postwar suburban America. In the film, Kimble's character represents a more explicit fear and sense of powerlessness in light of the immense growth and dominance of global capitalism and multinational corporations in everyday life.

Coda

As a popular American television series, *The Fugitive* reflected the cultural times in which it was produced. The series, which features the trials and tribulations of an innocent man hunted by his own society, seemed to touch a sympathetic chord with the American public. *The Fugitive* expresses the underlying anxieties of many Americans about the frailty of America's postwar middle class in a society of increased institutional and corporate bureaucratization. Kimble's travels contradictorily speak to the implicit desire of bourgeois Americans for liberation and escape from the social confines and conformity of suburban America. The road is both a renewable source of individual freedom and a noir nightmare. The series also articulates a concern over the loss of personal identity and autonomy in modern capitalist society built on increasing the efficiencies and control of both market and state powers. Lawrence Laurent (1964) contends that *The Fugitive*'s premise of an innocent man on the run who is able to change his identity at will challenges society's desire to control personal identity through such means as fingerprinting and Social Security numbers. The series' social concern over the loss of personal identity and control becomes more relevant today with the increased proliferation of corporate and governmental databases, surveillance, and biological identification technologies (such as DNA typing). The injustices faced by Kimble, combined with his distrust of authority, indirectly associate him with minorities and other social groups who were or would be struggling for social justice throughout the 1960s. Peder J. Zane says that *The Fugitive* was "the most daring and subversive network series ever broadcast," for while most prime-time series were playing it safe, Kimble's trials expressed "the broad discontent, the mistrust of authority and the concern for the downtrodden that were blossoming in the 1960s" (2007). Kimble's long, fateful journey perfectly captured the country's growing alienation and disenchantment during those increasingly volatile years. *The Fugitive*, as one of the most memorable and influential series on American television, established the essential narrative and thematic characteristics that would make the television wanderer-redeemer tradition the most enduring and meaningful form in television history.

NOTES

1. The first nonviolent, "contemporary" wanderer-redeemer TV series was *Route 66* (1960–64) on CBS. Roy Huggins's antiheroic Bret Maverick (James Garner) on the ABC western series *Maverick* (1957–62) provided the first cracks in breaking the dominance of the self-sacrificing, super-violent redeemer in TV westerns. These cracks, coupled with an oversaturation of action-adventure programming and federal regulatory pressures, laid the foundation for the creation of *The Fugitive* and other nonviolent wanderer-redeemer series.
2. The *Bus Stop* episode "A Lion Walks among Us" (12/2/61) featured pop singer Fabian as an amoral psychotic killer. ABC president Oliver Treyz later admitted that he had been guilty of poor judgment in allowing the episode to air. For further information, see Barnouw 1990, 303–6.
3. W. T. Lhamon (1990) argues that the 1950s were not a bland cultural period but set the intellectual and stylistic tone for the decades to follow. In his analysis of 1950s popular culture, especially rock n' roll music, he finds strong impulses and echoes of America's attempts to transform itself from an industrial to a post-industrial society. Lhamon asserts that the breakdown of racial barriers through popular culture was the central cause of the decade's "postmodern revolution."
4. The final marital struggle between Richard and Helen Kimble was over his desire to adopt a child. In his fugitive travels, Kimble is able to serve as a surrogate parent and protector of children.

Notes

5. Levy states that *The Chase* (1966) and *Easy Rider* (1969) both portray small towns as seething hotbeds of racial, class, and social conflicts often involving distinct tensions between social groups: "parents versus children . . . dominant culture versus subversive counterculture" (1991, 172–73).

WORKS CITED

Alvey, Robert. 1997. "Wanderlust and Wire Wheels: The Existential Search of *Route 66*." In *The Road Film Book*, ed. Steven Cohan and Ina Rae Hark, 143–64. New York: Routledge.

———. 2011. "The Defenders." Museum of Broadcast Communications. http://www.museum.tv/eotvsection.php?entrycode=defendersth (accessed March 10, 2011).

Anderson, Christopher. 1994. *HollywoodTV: The Studio System in the Fifties*. Austin: University of Texas Press.

———. "Huggins, Roy, U.S. Producer." 1997. In *The Museum of Broadcast Communications Encyclopedia of Television*, ed. Horace Newcomb, vol. 2, G–P, 807–8. Chicago: Fitzroy Dearborn.

Ang, Ien. 1996. "Melodramatic Identifications: Television Fiction and Women's Fantasy." In *Living Room War: Rethinking Media Audiences for a Postmodern World,* ed. Ien Ang, 72–82. New York: Routledge.

Ayres, C. E. 1965. "The Case for Technology." In *Issues of the Sixties, 1965–1970*, 2nd ed., ed. Leonard Freedman, 9–13. Belmont, CA: Wadsworth.

Barnouw, Erik. 1990. *Tube of Plenty: The Evolution of American Television*. 2nd ed. New York: Oxford University Press.

Bellah, Robert N., Richard Madsen, William M. Sullivan, Ann Swidler, and Steven M. Tipton. 1985. *Habits of the Heart: Individualism and Commitment in American Life*. New York: Harper.

Bledstein, Burton J. 1976. *The Culture of Professionalism*. New York: Norton.

Britton, Andrew. 1986. "Blissing Out: The Politics of Reaganite Entertainment." *Movie* 31:32, 1–42.

Brooks, Peter. 1976. *The Melodramatic Imagination: Balzac, Henry James, Melodrama, and the Mode of Excess*. New Haven, CT: Yale University Press.

Brooks, Tim, and Earle Marsh. 1988. *The Complete Directory to Prime Time Network TV Shows, 1946–Present*. 4th ed. New York: Ballantine.

Broughton, Irv, ed. 1986. *Producers on Producing: The Making of Film and Television*. Jefferson, NC: McFarland.

Buhle, Paul, and Dave Wagner. 2003. *Hide in Plain Sight: The Hollywood Blacklistees in Film and Television, 1950–2002*. New York: Palgrave-Macmillan.

Castleman, Harry, and Walter J. Podrazik. 1982. *Watching TV: Four Decades of American Television*. New York: McGraw-Hill.

Clecak, Peter. 1983. *America's Quest for the Ideal Self*. New York: Oxford University Press.

Cook, Fred J. 1961. "The Scales of Justice." *The Nation* 198 (August 12): 84–85.

Cooper, John. 1997. "Quinn Martin, U.S. Producer." In *The Museum of Broadcast Communications Encyclopedia of Television*, ed. Horace Newcomb, vol. 2, G–P, 1004–5. Chicago: Fitzroy Dearborn.

Durgnat, Raymond. 1996. "Paint It Black: The Family Tree of the Film Noir." In *Film Noir Reader*, ed. Alain Silver and James Ursini, 37–51. New York: Limelight.

Ehrenreich, Barbara. 1983. *The Hearts of Men: American Dreams and the Flight from Commitment*. Garden City, NY: Anchor/Doubleday.

Eliot, Marc. 1981. *American Television: The Official Art of the Artificial*. Garden City, NY: Anchor Bay/Doubleday.

Ellul, Jacques. 1964. *The Technological Society*. New York: Knopf.

Finestone, Aaron. 2009. "Shooting Pool with David Goodis." http://www.davidgoodis.com/page1/page15/page15.html (accessed July 23, 2010).

Fiske, John. 1984. "Popularity and Ideology: A Structuralist Reading of *Dr. Who*." In *Interpreting Television: Current Research Perspectives*, ed. Willard D. Rowland Jr. and Bruce Watkins, 165–89. Beverly Hills, CA: Sage.

———. 1987. *Television Culture*. London: Methuen.

Frankel, Charles. 1964. "Is It Ever Right to Break the Law?" *New York Times Magazine*, January 12, p. 17.

Friedan, Betty. 1963. 2001. *The Feminine Mystique*. New York: Norton.
"The Fuge." 1965. *Newsweek*, April 26, p. 94.
"The Fugitive." Box Office Mojo. http://www.boxofficemojo.com/movies/?id=fugitive.htm (accessed July 22, 2009).
Fulbright, William J. 1965. "Space: Why the Crash Program?" In *Issues of the Sixties, 1965–1970*, 2nd ed., ed. Leonard Freedman, 33–36. Belmont, CA: Wadsworth.
Glover, Allen, and David Bushman. 2006. "Lights Out in the Wasteland: The TV Noir." *Television Quarterly* 37:1, 67–75.
Goldenson, Leonard H., with Marvin J. Wolf. 1991. *Beating the Odds: The Untold Story behind the Rise of ABC: The Stars, Struggles, and Egos That Transformed Network Television by the Man Who Made It Happen*. New York: Scribner's.
Goldwater, Barry. 1965. "Our Moral Strength Has Declined." In *Issues of the Sixties, 1965–1970*, 2nd ed., ed. Leonard Freeman, 380–81. Belmont, CA: Wadsworth.
Goodis, David. 1946, 1999. *Dark Passage*. London: Prion Books.
Gould, Jack. 1963. "TV: Discharge of Treyz." *New York Times*, April 21, sec. 17:2.
———. 1969. "TV Review: Three New Shows and a Local Documentary." *New York Times*, September 18, sec. 95:1.
Grossman, Kathryn M. 1994. *Figuring Transcendence in "Les Misérables," Hugo's Romantic Sublime*. Carbondale: Southern Illinois University Press.
Guitar, Mary Ann. 1963. "I Want to Be an Amateur." *Mademoiselle* (October): 152–84.
Hesburgh, Theodore M. 1963. "Science Is Amoral; Need Scientists Be Amoral Too?" *Saturday Review,* March 2, pp. 55–57.
Himmelstein, Hal. 1984. *Television Myth and the American Mind*. New York: Praeger.
Holmes, Paul. 1961. *The Sheppard Murder Case*. New York: Bantam Books.
Huggins, Roy. 1998. Interview by Lee Goldberg. Archive of American Television, July 21. http://www.emmytvlegends.org/interviews/people/roy-huggins (accessed July 15, 2010).
Jacques, Elliot. 1965. "Death and the Mid-life Crisis." *International Journal of Psychoanalysis* 46:502–14.
Jameson, Frederic. 1992. *The Geopolitical Aesthetic: Cinema and Space in the World System*. Bloomington: Indiana University Press.
Jewett, Robert, and John Shelton Lawrence. 1977. *The American Mono-*

myth. Garden City, NY: Anchor Press/Doubleday.

Kerouac, Jack. 1957, 1965. *On the Road*. New York: Viking Press.

Kravitz, Bennett. 1999. "The Truth Is Out There: Conspiracy as a Mindset in American High and Popular Culture." *Journal of American Culture* 22:4, pp. 23–29.

Laurent, Lawrence. 1964. "'Fugitive' Escapes Capture by Ratings." *Washington Post*, April 23, p. D17.

Leitch, Thomas. 2005. *Perry Mason*. Detroit: Wayne State University Press.

Levy, Emanuel. 1991. *Small-Town America in Film: The Decline and Fall of Community*. New York: Continuum.

Lhamon, W. T. 1990. *Deliberate Speed: The Origins of a Cultural Style in the American 1950s*. Washington, DC: Smithsonian Institution Press.

Malsbary, Robert, Robert G. Strange Jr., and Lynn Wooley. 1985. *Warner Bros. Television*. Jefferson, NC: McFarland.

Marc, David, and Robert J. Thompson. 1992. *Prime Time, Prime Movers: From "I Love Lucy" to "L.A. Law"—America's Greatest TV Shows and the People Who Created Them*. Boston: Little, Brown.

Mills, C. Wright. 1970. *The Power Elite*. New York: Oxford University Press.

Minow, Newton N. 1961. "Television and the Public Interest." American Rhetoric, Top 100 Speeches. http://www.americanrhetoric.com/speeches/newtonminow.htm (accessed July 22, 2010).

Mintz, Steven, and Susan Kellogg. 1988. *Domestic Revolutions: A Social History of American Family Life*. New York: The Free Press, 1988.

Moriz, Charles, ed. 1967. "Janssen, David." *Current Biography 1967*. New York: H. W. Wilson.

Newcomb, Horace. 1974. *TV: The Most Popular Art*. Garden City, NY: Anchor Press.

Newcomb, Horace, and Robert S. Alley. 1983. *The Producer's Medium*. New York: Oxford University Press.

O'Connor, John. 1980. "David Janssen—The Model Actor." *New York Times*, March 30, pp. 43–44.

———. 1984. "TV Reviews: Highway to Heaven with Landon." *New York Times*, September 19, sec. C26:1.

———. 1989. "Review: Television—An Actor's Quantum Leap through Time and Roles." *New York Times*, November 22, sec. 18:5.

O'Donnell, Victoria. 2007. *Television Criticism*. London: Sage.

Orlick, Peter. "Have Gun, Will Travel." Museum of Broadcast Communications. http://www.museum.tv/archives/etv/H/htmlH/havengunwil/

havegunwil.htm (accessed July 15, 2010).

Polenburg, Richard. 1980. *One Nation Divisible: Class, Race and Ethnicity in the United States since 1938*. New York: Viking.

Porfirio, Robert G. 1996. "No Way Out: Existential Motifs in the Film Noir." In *Film Noir Reader*, ed. Alain Silver and James Ursini, 77–93. New York: Limelight.

Proctor, Mel. 1994. *The Official Fan's Guide to the Fugitive*. Stamford, CT: Longmeadow Press.

Rapping, Elayne. 2006. *Law and Justice as Seen on TV*. New York: New York University Press.

Rapson, Richard. 1988. *American Yearning: Love, Money & Endless Possibility*. Lanham, MD: University Press of America.

Rathwell, Mark. 1998. "An Introduction to *The Incredible Hulk*." http://www.incrediblehulktvseries.com/Intro/Hulkintro.htm (accessed July 22, 2009).

Rickover, H. G. 1963. "The Decline of the Individual." *Saturday Evening Post*, March 30, pp. 11–13.

Robertson, Ed. 1993. *The Fugitive, Recaptured*. Los Angeles: Pomegranate Press.

Schatz, Thomas. 1991. "The Family Melodrama." In *Imitations of Life: A Reader of Film and Television Melodrama*, ed. Marcia Landy, 148–67. Detroit: Wayne State University Press.

Schmidt, Lisa. 2010. "Monstrous Melodrama: Expanding the Scope of Melodramatic Identification to Interpret Negative Fan Responses to *Supernatural*." *Transformative Works and Cultures*, vol. 4, http://journal.transformativeworks.org/index.php/twc/article/viewArticle/152/155 (accessed August 10, 2010).

Schrader, Paul. 2003. "Notes on Film Noir." In *Film Genre Reader III*, 3rd ed., ed. Barry Keith Grant, 229–43. Austin: University of Texas Press.

Spicer, Andrew. 2002. *Film Noir*. New York: Longman.

Sterngold, James. 1997. "A Fellowship of Angels and America." *New York Times*, April 6.

Sullivan, William M. 1995. *Work and Integrity: The Crisis and Promise of Professionalism in America*. New York: HarperBusiness.

Swidler, Ann. 1980. "Love and Adulthood in American Culture." In *Themes of Work and Love in Adulthood*, ed. Neil Smelser and Erik Erikson, 115–42. Cambridge, MA: Harvard University Press.

Thorburn, David. 1977. "Homage to David Janssen." In *TV Book*, ed. Judy Freeman, 192–93. New York: Workman.

Ursini, James. 1996. "Angst at Sixty Fields per Second." In *Film Noir Reader*, ed. Alain Silver and James Ursini, 275–87. New York: Limelight.

Vahimagi, Tise. 1997. "The Fugitive, U.S. Adventure/Melodrama." *Museum of Broadcast Communications Encyclopedia of Television*, ed. Horace Newcomb, vol. 1, A–F, 655. Chicago: Fitzroy Dearborn.

Watson, Mary Ann. 1990. *Expanding Vista: American Television in the Kennedy Years*. New York: Oxford University Press.

Whyte, William H. 1956. *The Organization Man*. Garden City, NY: Doubleday.

Wood, Robin. 1986. *Hollywood from Vietnam to Reagan*. New York: Columbia University Press.

Zane, Peder J. 2007. "Kimble, Nation Went on the Run." Knight Ridder Tribune News Service, August 28, p. 1.

FILM

All That Heaven Allows (Douglas Sirk 1955)
Back to the Future (Robert Zemekis 1985)
The Big Heat (Fritz Lang 1953)
The Big Operator (Charles Haas 1959)
The Chase (Arthur Penn 1966)
Dark Passage (Delmer Daves 1947)
Double Indemnity (Billy Wilder 1944)
Easy Rider (Dennis Hooper 1969)
E.T.: The Extra-Terrestrial (Steven Spielberg 1982)
Force of Evil (Abraham Polonsky 1948)
The Fugitive (Andrew Davis 1993)
The Godfather (Francis Ford Coppola 1972)
Hangman's Knot (Roy Huggins 1952)
Here Comes Mr. Jordan (Alexander Hall 1941)
Human Desire (Fritz Lang 1954)
The International (Tom Tykwer 2009)
I Was a Communist for the F.B.I. (Gordon Douglas 1951)
My Son John (Leo McCarey 1952)
Peggy Sue Got Married (Francis Ford Coppola 1986)
Peyton Place (Mark Robson 1957)
Picnic (Joshua Logan 1955)
Raiders of the Lost Ark (Steven Spielberg 1981)
Rear Window (Alfred Hitchcock 1954)
Requiem for a Heavyweight (Ralph Nelson 1962)

Film

Star Wars (George Lucas 1977)
Superman (Richard Donner 1978)
They Live by Night (Nicholas Ray 1949)
Walk East on Beacon Street (Alfred Werker 1952)
The Wild Angels (Roger Corman 1966)
The Wrong Man (Alfred Hitchcock 1956)
You Only Live Once (Fritz Lang 1937)

TELEVISION

The A-Team (NBC, 1983–87)
Barnaby Jones (CBS, 1973–80)
Beauty and the Beast (CBS, 1987–90)
Ben Casey (ABC, 1961–66)
Branded (NBC, 1965–66)
The Breaking Point (ABC, 1963–64)
Bus Stop (ABC, 1961–62)
Cannon (CBS, 1971–76)
Channing (ABC, 1963–64)
Cheers (NBC, 1982–93)
Cheyenne (ABC, 1955–63)
China Smith (syndicated, 1952–54)
Colt .45 (ABC, 1957–63)
Crime Story (NBC, 1986–88)
Dallas (CBS, 1978–91)
Dante (NBC, 1960–61)
The Defenders (CBS, 1961–65)
Dragnet (NBC, 1951–59, 1967–70, 1989–91)
Dr. Kildare (NBC, 1961–66)
The F.B.I. (ABC, 1965–74)
The Fugitive (ABC, 1963–67)
The Fugitive (CBS, 2000–2001)
Have Gun Will Travel (CBS, 1957–63)
Highway to Heaven (NBC, 1984–89)

The Howdy Doody Show (NBC, 1947–60)
The Immortal (ABC, 1970–71)
The Incredible Hulk (CBS, 1978–82)
The Invaders (ABC, 1967–68)
It's the Garry Shandling Show (Showtime, 1986–90)
Johnny Staccato (NBC, 1959–60)
Kraft Television Theatre (NBC, 1947–58; ABC, 1953–55)
Late Night with David Letterman (NBC, 1982–93)
Leave It to Beaver (CBS, 1957–58; ABC, 1958–63)
The Loner (CBS, 1965–66)
Magnum, P.I. (CBS, 1980–88)
A Man Called Shenandoah (ABC, 1965–66)
The Man with a Camera (ABC, 1958–60)
The Many Loves of Dobie Gillis (CBS, 1959–63)
Mary Tyler Moore Show (CBS, 1970–77)
*M*A*S*H* (CBS, 1972–83)
Maverick (ABC, 1957–62)
Mickey Spillane's Mike Hammer (CBS, 1958–59)
Mr. Novak (NBC, 1963–65)
Naked City (ABC, 1958–63)
N.C.I.S. (CBS, 2003–present)
The New Breed (ABC, 1961–62)
Nowhere Man (UPN, 1995–96)
Perry Mason (CBS, 1957–66)
Peter Gunn (NBC, 1958–61)
Playhouse 90 (CBS, 1955–61)
The Pretender (NBC, 1996–2000)
Prison Break (Fox, 2005–9)
Promised Land (CBS, 1996–99)
Quantum Leap (NBC, 1989–93)
Renegade (syndicated, 1992–97)
Richard Diamond, Private Detective (1957–60)
Route 66 (CBS, 1960–64)
Run, Buddy, Run (CBS, 1966–67)
Run for Your Life (NBC, 1965–68)
77 Sunset Strip (ABC, 1958–64)
The Simpsons (Fox, 1989–present)
Starman (ABC, 1986–87)
The Streets of San Francisco (ABC, 1972–77)

Then Came Bronson (NBC, 1969–70)
Touched by an Angel (CBS, 1994–2003)
Twelve O'Clock High (ABC, 1964–67)
The Twilight Zone (CBS, 1959–64)
Twin Peaks (ABC, 1990–91)
The Untouchables (ABC, 1959–63)
Wagon Train (NBC, 1957–62; ABC, 1962–65)
Warner Bros. Presents (ABC, 1955–56)
Wiseguy (CBS, 1987–90)

INDEX

American Broadcasting Company
  (ABC): creation of *The Fugitive*,
  9, 11–12, 14, 35; response to
  regulatory climate, 9, 23, 31, 97.
  See also Goldenson, Leonard
American justice system, 16, 22,
  44; critique of, 66, 67, 69–70;
  liberalization, 66–67. *See also*
  Warren Court
Anderson, Richard, 30
Arab oil embargo, 74–75
Armer, Alan, 21
Arts & Entertainment Network, 8–9
authority, 10, 66, 70–72; distrust of,
  71, 72, 95

Bacall, Lauren, 17
Bakula, Scott, 86, 87
Beat movement, 25, 27–28, 43, 47
Bellisario, Donald P., 86
Berry, Chuck, 41
Bertinelli, Valerie, 89
Big Heat, The (Fritz Lang), 73
Bixby, Bill, 83
Bogart, Humphrey, 17

Brando, Marlon, 41
Bruce, Lenny, 43
Bus Stop (William Inge), 2n97, 23,
  29–30

Camus, Albert, 4
capitalism, corporate, 42, 73, 91,
  94; global, 92, 92–93, 94
Chase, The (Arthur Penn), 5n98, 70
Cheyenne, 23, 24
children: leaving home, 45; Kimble
  as surrogate parent, 4n97, 27, 51
civil rights movement, 33, 56,
  71–72
cold war, 4, 22–23, 35–36, 39; *The
  Fugitive* as critique of, 35–36
Columbia Pictures, 13
Colvin, Jack, 83–84
Conrad, William, 2, 36, 77
countercultural movement, 3n97,
  41, 43, 74, 79, 82
Crucible, The (Arthur Miller), 46

Dallas, 7
Dark Passage, 17–18

Davis, Andrew, 9, 90
Dean, James, 1, 41
Defenders, The, 8, 31–32, 67
Dodd congressional hearings, 23
Double Indemnity (Billy Wilder), 35
Downey, Roma, 88
Dragnet, 2
Dye, John, 88–89

Easy Rider (Dennis Hopper), 5n97, 70
Ehrenreich, Barbara, 49, 52
Ellul, Jacques, 63–64

family: ambivalence to, 89; as spiritual balm, 89
F.B.I., The, 20, 22
Feminine Mystique, The, 49
Ferrigno, Lou, 83
Force of Evil (Abraham Polonsky), 73
Ford, Glenn, 73
Ford, Harrison, 9, 90, 94
French, Victor, 85
Friedan, Betty, 49
Fugitive, The (ABC): as existential series, 4, 34–35; final episode, 7, 77; generic roots of, 24–37; guest stars, 30–31, 33; as melodrama, 26–27; as *noir* series (*see* TV noir); parodies of, 6, 8; pilot episode, 18–19; popularity of, 1–2, 8, 9; program imitators, 6
Fugitive, The (CBS), 9
Fugitive, The (movie), 8–9, 10, 14; as conspiratorial thriller, 91, 92–93; similarities and differences to the TV series, 93–94
Fulbright, William J., 64

Garfield, John, 73

Gazzara, Ben, 78, 79, 82
Gerard, Philip (ABC series character): as husband, 54–55; as middle-class professional, 57–58; as "obsessive" police detective, 2, 3, 16, 17, 22, 57–58, 59, 91; as an "organization man," 57; as parent, 58; similarities to Hugo's Javert, 16
Ginsberg, Allen, 41
Godfather, The (Francis Ford Coppola), 73
Goldenson, Leonard, 11, 12, 23
Goldwater, Barry, 42–43
Goodis, David, 17–18

Hangman's Knot (Roy Huggins), 12
Have Gun Will Travel, 24–25
Highway to Heaven, 7, 75, 78, 84–85, 86, 88
Hollywood blacklisting, 15–16, 67
House Un-American Activities Committee (HUAC), 15–16
Huggins, Roy: creator of *The Fugitive,* 1n97, 6, 9, 11–12, 14, 18–19, 23, 25, 35, 39; creator of *Run for Your Life,* 78; early career, 12–13; rebuttal to Minow's speech, 23
Human Desire (Fritz Lang), 35
humanism, secular, 17
humanistic perspective, 63, 74

Incredible Hulk, The, 7, 75, 83–84
individualism, 10, 42, 46, 48–49, 72; expressive, 43–44, 45, 47, 82; loss of, 42, 43, 95; middle-class, 44; mythic, 44; radical, 47, 48; and realism, 45–46
International, The, 92–93

Janssen, David: acting in *The Fugitive,* 1, 3–4, 20, 82; early career, 3, 20; relationship to Quinn Martin, 20
Johnson, Lyndon B., 42–43
Jones, Tommy Lee, 9, 90–91

Kennedy, John F., 3, 25, 28, 56
Kerouac, Jack, 25, 41. *See also* Beat movement
Kimble, Richard (ABC series character): as alienated "victim-hero," 4, 35, 41, 43–44, 56, 79, 95–96; as husband, 4n97, 15, 48, 50–51, 53; as middle-class professional, 35, 50, 57; as physician, 14, 33, 35, 58, 64, 66; similarities to Goodis's Parry, 17–18; similarities to Hugo's Valjean, 16, 17; as wanderer-redeemer (*see* wanderer-redeemer tradition); as western hero, 25
King, Martin Luther Jr., 71

Landon, Michael, 84, 85
love, romantic, 10, 49
Lynch, David (*Twin Peaks*), 8

Maharis, George, 25
marriage: and divorce, 48, 49, 54; effects of careerism on, 55, 56, 57; Gerard's marriage, 54–55; Kimble's marriage, 27, 48; as social institution, 10, 48–49, 50; social pressures on, 48–49
Martin, Quinn: early career, 19, 20; endorsement of conservative ideals, 22, 54; as producer of *The Fugitive,* 7, 9, 14, 18–19, 21, 36–37; as prolific TV producer, 19–20. *See also* Q.M. Productions

Maverick, 1n97, 12–13
McCarthy, Lin, 30
McCarthyism, 4, 39
melodrama, family, 26–27
men: flight from male provider image, 49–50; *The Fugitive* as flight from male provider image, 50; married men as predatory beasts, 52; social sanctions against men, 52
midlife crisis, 54
Mills, C. Wright, 42, 62
Milner, Martin, 25
Minow's "Vast Wasteland" speech, 9, 22–23
Misérables, Les (Victor Hugo), 16–18, 83–84
Morse, Barry, 2, 3, 16
Mr. Novak, 8

Naked City, 29
New Breed, The, 18
New Frontier administration, 3, 28–29; liberalism, 3, 5, 25, 33, 56
New Frontier professional dramas, 31–32; African American actors, 33; "Civil Rights TV Season," 33; *The Fugitive's* similarities and differences to, 32–34

Parks, Michael, 81, 82
Perry Mason, 67
Presley, Elvis, 41
professionalism, culture of, 3, 10, 56; conflict with professional ethics, 58, 60–63; distrust of, 56; Kimble and Gerard as professionals, 57–58; middle-class professionalism, 35, 56, 57

Q.M. Productions, 2, 8, 13, 14, 18, 19; in-house production style, 2, 20–22, 22, 37, 39. *See also* Martin, Quinn
Quantum Leap, 7, 75, 83, 86–88, 90

Raisch, Bill, 30
Reagan, Ronald W.: historical revisionism, 88
Reaganite entertainment, 82–83, 88, 91
Rear Window (Alfred Hitchcock), 36
Reese, Della, 88
Reisman, David, 42
Richard Diamond, Private Detective, 20
road as symbol: for the Beats, 27–28; for the New Frontier, 28–29; source of liberation, 95; source of *noir* nightmare, 95
Rooney, Mickey, 30–31
Route 66, 1n97, 25–26, 27, 85
Rugolo, Peter, 2, 27
Run for Your Life, 6, 78–81

science, modern, and technology: 10, 63; critique of, 63–64; as destructive force, 65–66; humanistic perspective, 63; as progressive force, 63, 65
scientist, representation of, 64–65, 66
Scott, Jacqueline, 30
semi-anthology series: definition of, 29; *The Fugitive* as a, 30; weakness of, 30
77 Sunset Strip, 12, 13
Sheppard, Murder Case, The, 14–15; similarities and differences to *The Fugitive,* 15
small-town America: critique of, 33, 46–47, 70, 73, 74, 98; extremism and vigilante justice, 70; social conformity, 33, 45, 46–47; social prejudice and corruption, 5n97, 72–73, 74
social justice, 10, 41, 66, 67–69, 70–71, 95
Stockwell, Dean, 86, 87
suburban America, 4, 26, 27, 40, 43, 93, 94, 95

television western: cowboy as violent redeemer, 1n97, 24 (*see also* wanderer-redeemer tradition); "excessive violence," 23; *The Fugitive* as western, 25, 66; "motorized western," 81; oversaturation of westerns, 1n97, 22–23; waning of westerns, 26
Then Came Bronson, 7, 81–82
Thoreau, Henry David, 43, 47
Touched by an Angel, 7, 88–90
20th Century Fox Studios, 12, 13
TV noir: history of, 34; innocent man on the run theme, 34, 39; *The Fugitive* as *noir* series, 34–35, 36–39

United Artist Television, 18
Untouchables, The, 9, 19
urban America, 47, 52, 73, 81–82, 94
Vietnam War, 74–75, 86, 88

Wagon Train, 29
Wallace, George C., 71
wanderer-redeemer tradition, 1n97, 6–7, 40, 75, 77–78, 81, 82–85, 86–90, 93–94, 96; fantasy wanderer-redeemer, 75, 82, 91; Judeo-Christian redeemer, 24,

78, 84, 94; nonviolent redeemer, 6, 10, 24, 25, 77, 84; violent redeemer, 24, 25, 84. *See also* television western
Ward, Sela, 90
Warner, Jack, 13, 20
Warner Bros. Presents, 12
Warner Bros. Studios, 8–9, 13, 90
Warren Court, 66–67
Watergate scandal, 74–75, 91
Weld, Tuesday, 31, 32
Whitman, Walt, 43, 45
Whyte, William, 42, 57
Wild Angels, The, 81
Williamson, Martha, 88
Winchell, Walter, 19
women: discontent as housewife, 49; patriarchal view of women, 47, 53; as romantic interest, 27, 53
working class, 30, 56